NEGOTIATE
YOUR JOB
OFFER

*A Step-by-Step Guide to a
Win-Win Situation*

NEGOTIATE
YOUR JOB
OFFER

MARY B. SIMON

JOHN WILEY & SONS, INC.

New York • Chichester • Weinheim • Brisbane • Singapore • Toronto

This text is printed on acid-free paper.

Copyright © 1998 by Mary B. Simon
Published by John Wiley & Sons, Inc.

This publication is designed to provide accurate and authoritative
information in regard to the subject matter covered. It is sold
with the understanding that the publisher is not engaged in
rendering legal, accounting, or other professional services. If
legal advice or other expert assistance is required, the services
of a competent professional person should be sought.

Library of Congress Cataloging-in-Publication Data:

Simon, Mary, 1957–
    Negotiate your job offer : a step-by-step guide to a win-win
situation / Mary Simon.
        p.   cm.
    Includes bibliographical references.
    ISBN 0-471-17185-9 (pbk. : alk. paper)
    1. Employment interviewing.   2. Job offers.   3. Negotiation in
business.   I. Title.
    HF5549.5.I6S55   1997
    650.14—dc21   97-26314

Printed in the United States of America

10 9 8 7 6 5 4 3 2 1

To Katherine Mary

and

"Aunt Kay"

Acknowledgments

The writing of this book has involved a *sculpting* process. Years spent living in other countries revealed the need to be flexible and willing to remain open in the face of differences and unexpected occurrences.

My ideas about negotiation began to take shape in my work as a faculty/staff member in the Wharton School of Business at the University of Pennsylvania and as a leader of *seminars* that drew large flocks of negotiators in the rough. These experiences were followed by important exchanges and work with all levels of professionals from Procter & Gamble, Scott Paper Company, IBM, Du Pont, Lockheed Martin, Martin Marietta, General Electric, and the Nuclear Regulatory Commission who struggled with maneuvering the complicated maze of career transition and settling on appropriate terms of agreement.

I observed the power of a well-crafted negotiating strategy in innumerable cross-cultural and professional situations. Hard though it can be to *stay clear and balanced* about the real priorities on the issues side *and* the interpersonal side, after working through the details of complex agreements, the power of the process and accurate, appropriate preparation became evident to me.

From a roughly outlined concept, this resulting book has become a testament to the *value of teamwork* and insightful support. Michele Brown has lent her skill, intelligence, talent, dedication, and grace; Janet Long has probed every syllable for accuracy and thorough, strong expression and has contributed Chapter 12, "Working and Negotiating through an Executive Search Firm." Ann Sheara came into the project with clarity, artistic strength, and an extraordinary ability to put form, structure, and priorities in place; Pat Davis lent her graphics talent to the original draft. I also extend a special thank-you to Robert Lipton for his thorough and professional review of the book contract.

I am grateful to Richard H. Beatty for the explicit and implicit endorsement for the publication of this book and for the steady professional care and support he consistently provides.

Thank you to those of you who graciously gave of your time in interviews.

Thank you to Mike Hamilton for his enthusiastic support and editorial guidance in bringing the final manuscript to completion. Essential to the strength, focus, and stamina required to produce this book have been my family and friends. This *nudge* team contributed the push and energy needed to keep chiseling away at the ideas. *Love and gratitude* go to my daughter, Katherine, to Kay, Bill, Sue, Rose, Pamela, Jim, Sharon, Esther, Alan, Jay, Eva, Dawn, Sherry, and Kathy.

Thank you to everyone for investing in something that I hope will be of value to many people in professional transition.

Contents

PART 2

DURING: Managing the Negotiation Process with Ease and Success

PART 3

AFTER: Bringing Closure to the Negotiation Process

APPENDIXES

What Negotiation Looks Like for Each of the Audiences

Introduction

People are always blaming their circumstances for what they are. I don't believe in circumstances. The people who get on in this world are the people who get up and look for circumstances they want, and if they can't find them—make them.

GEORGE BERNARD SHAW
MRS. WARREN'S PROFESSION

This book is meant to be a "can do" *wake-up call* for anyone at the last stage of a job change effort. Whereas fuzzy thinking interferes with a sense of ability when the final job offer is presented, with the right frame of mind and preparation, you can represent yourself well.

The last stage of a job search or job change process often involves some form of negotiation. Regardless of who you are, how knowledgeable and sophisticated you are, how savvy you are in your normal mode of work, *don't be surprised* if feelings of intimidation creep into your psyche when you must negotiate *on your own* behalf.

Not only is it harder to negotiate a job offer than to negotiate with a car salesperson about the price of a car, it is harder to negotiate your job offer than to negotiate as a representative for a service or a product. The reason is that when you are negotiating with a car salesperson, the focus is on the car, and on how crafty and capable you can be in bargaining with the salesperson. You can put your *gamesmanship* hat on and strategize in an objective way rather than in a deeply personal way.

The stakes get a little higher when you are negotiating as a representative of a service or product because a customer or client relationship is at issue, but you still have the luxury of being less involved on a personal level, which allows you to maintain an objective stance.

Preserving the relationship with the client requires you to be more sensitive to careful communication, but the *protective barrier* of being able to stand behind the service or product line affords you a buffer that isn't there when you are negotiating on your own behalf about the terms of a job offer. The degree of difficulty increases as you enter this arena of self-representation. Don't be put off by any visceral reaction you might experience. In the pages of this book, I have given you everything you need to manage a smooth, effective negotiation. All the exercises, questions, scripts, and real-life examples or cases are meant to be user-friendly and impactful. I know from personal experience how awkward it can be to enter this zone of negotiation. I also know that you can transform the awkwardness into confidence, and this book shows how to maneuver the process with skill, ease, and confidence.

Common to every job offer negotiation situation are:

Listening Skills	Investigative Skills
Analytical ability	Courage
Assertiveness	Creativity
Courtesy	Focus
Decision-making ability	Follow-through
Detail orientation	Good eye contact
Objectivity	Interpersonal communication skills
Organization ability	Patience
Personal flexibility	Preparation
Problem-solving ability	Reality testing
Focused questioning	Self-marketing skills
Tenacity	Written communication skills
Tolerance for ambiguity	
Troubleshooting ability	

You do not have to be an expert in every skill area, but you need to be able to slow down long enough to figure out how to play your part in the negotiated exchange.

Among the skills and abilities you need to use, the following are the most important:

① Listening skills.
② Ability to ask good questions.

③ Personal flexibility.

④ Being courteous and extending yourself.

⑤ Ability to balance between the details of the offer while continuing to cultivate the relationship.

⑥ Assertiveness and self-marketing skills.

⑦ Problem-solving skills.

⑧ Organization skills.

⑨ Research skills.

⑩ Polite tenacity.

If you are strong in the top 5 skills, you will be able to do well; if you are strong in the top 8 skills, you should be able to do very well; and if you are strong in all 10 skill/ability areas, you should perform exceptionally well.

It is quite possible to become practiced in these techniques. Rehearse them with friends, with a salesperson, at home, or with colleagues. Good negotiation results from a combination of the 10 core skills.

| Chapters 1–10 |

Each of the core skills are addressed in the 20 chapters of the book and in the Appendixes. Chapters 1 through 10 involve the *analysis, evaluation,* and *preparation* phases of the negotiation. They cover everything from outlining your career priorities, to understanding the needs, goals, and perspectives of employers when they are constructing an offer, to deciding when and when not to pursue negotiation.

| Chapters 11–20 |

Chapters 11 through 20 involve actual *management of the negotiation process.* Chapters include diverse topics such as: mastering negotiation skills, working with executive recruiters, separating personal and business issues and considering creative total compensation terms.

Finally, offer letters and letters declining an offer are included as well as three appendixes that address special negotiation concerns for those who need to make connections between the interview process and the final negotiation, the person affected by downsizing, and for graduate students.

If you are in a hurry, the *Agenda and Action Items* sections in every chapter allow you to find focused information with expedience. The stories illustrate real situations that have occurred during my 18 years of experience in this field, and the exercises are efficient, easy to complete, and easy to apply to your particular situation.

This book is designed to be a well-worn guide. Write on its pages to your heart's content!

PART 1

BEFORE

Analysis, Evaluation, and Preparation

| CHAPTER **1** | *Establishing Job/Career Selection Priorities* |

Agenda

- Working on a *Career Priority Self-Inventory.*

- Tom's Story *(a project leader for a large company decides to work for a small, start-up company).*

- Maria's Story *(evaluating an offer against her core criteria).*

- Staying grounded in what is important to you.

Give to us clear vision that we may know where to stand and what to stand for—because unless we stand for something, we shall fall for anything.

PETER MARSHALL, SENATE CHAPLAIN
PRAYER OFFERED AT THE OPENING OF THE SESSION,
APRIL 18, 1947, SEN. DOC. 8–170

Date: Today

To: Everyone Who Wants to Know *Where to Start*

Subject: Beginning the Process with a Complete Self-Inventory

---

What is of critical importance to you as you think about a transition into a new environment? It may have been a long time since you worked on a roster of quality of life and professional items that represent your priorities. Maybe you have never had the need to assemble this kind of information and things have just come together for you in a natural, easy fashion.

Do not be intimidated: The step-by-step process described in these pages will take the mystique out of preparing for a negotiation by breaking it into logical, digestible—and most of all—manageable pieces. Apply as much as you can from each of the 20 chapters and enjoy the chance to prepare for something that is important to *you!*

Figuring out what is important to you and why, takes some thinking and examination of your motivations, values, professional aspirations, and experiences.

WHAT IS IMPORTANT TO YOU?

Use the Career Priority Self-Inventory on pages 4–5 to prompt your thoughts. Put a check mark (✓) in the box next to each item that is important to you. Indicate how much you value the item by ranking it from 1 to 10 *(1 = lowest, 10 = highest)* in the "Personal Rating" column. Then, in the "Potential Offer" column, weigh the offer you are considering and give it *(or the potential for an offer, derived from what you know so far about the company and the position)* a 1 to 10 rating *(1= lowest, 10 = highest)* based on how well you perceive it stacks up against each priority you have checked and ranked in personal importance. Add to the list as you see fit. You can avoid the temptation to put a check mark (✓) by every item by realizing that you can only select between 8 and 10 priorities. Be truthful with yourself.

CAREER PRIORITY SELF-INVENTORY

	✓	Personal Rating 1–10	Potential Offer 1–10
1. Quality of work environment.	☐	○	☐
2. Title.	☐	○	☐
3. Ability for me to use my skills, training, and experience.	☐	○	☐
4. Corporate culture.	☐	○	☐
5. Length of commute.	☐	○	☐
6. Type of company.	☐	○	☐
7. Type of industry.	☐	○	☐
8. Opportunity to grow professionally.	☐	○	☐
9. Opportunity to work in an entrepreneurial environment.	☐	○	☐
10. Opportunity to work in a start-up environment.	☐	○	☐
11. Opportunity to work in a team-oriented environment.	☐	○	☐
12. Work in a new industry.	☐	○	☐
13. Work in a large corporation.	☐	○	☐
14. Use a company car.	☐	○	☐
15. Have the flexibility to work from home once a week.	☐	○	☐
16. Have the opportunity to work with new project requirements.	☐	○	☐
17. Have a nice office.	☐	○	☐
18. Work in a family-friendly environment.	☐	○	☐

(continued)

CAREER PRIORITY SELF-INVENTORY (CONTINUED)

	✓	Personal Rating 1–10	Potential Offer 1–10
19. Have on-site day care.	☐	○	☐
20. Be able to take advantage of tuition reimbursement benefits.	☐	○	☐
21. Increase my base pay and an overall good to above-average compensation package.	☐	○	☐
22. Receive an annual bonus.	☐	○	☐
23. Receive a sign-on bonus.	☐	○	☐
24. Be in an open, friendly environment.	☐	○	☐
25. Experience a fair amount of autonomy.	☐	○	☐
26. Travel a reasonable, not excessive, amount of time (15%–20%).	☐	○	☐
27. Be able to grow with the company without relocating.	☐	○	☐
28. Have a mentor or good career coach.	☐	○	☐
29. Have health club membership.	☐	○	☐
30.	☐	○	☐
31.	☐	○	☐
32.	☐	○	☐
33.	☐	○	☐
34.	☐	○	☐
35.	☐	○	☐
36.	☐	○	☐
37.	☐	○	☐
38.	☐	○	☐

Consider the following real-life experiences as you determine your own career priorities:

Tom's Story

Tom, a respected project leader at a manufacturing site of a Fortune 500 corporation, was facing an imminent separation from the company. His performance was recognized for consistently strong results and strong problem solving, but the site was slated to close the operation with which he was directly involved.

Tom conducted a careful survey of his work-related achievements and decided to look for another job in his immediate geographic area. Hard though it was to leave his company (he was offered the opportunity to transfer to another location), he determined that he had to balance his appreciation for the structure, resources, and opportunities in the company with some important priorities in his personal life.

He was the father of a young child and wanted to be more available to raise him than he had been. Seeing his child grow up so quickly made him wake up to the need for balance.

His work on the *Career Priority Self-Inventory* resulted in the following priorities shown on page 7.

After he evaluated his priorities, he launched a job search. Fortunately for him, he received an offer within a few months. A manufacturing start-up company within an hour from where he lived needed someone with his background. Because it was a start-up operation, he was not going to experience the same luxury of what often seemed like unlimited resources, but he was going to have an opportunity to assume new responsibilities and work from home one day a week. He also was going to be a central player in the operation and welcomed the chance to make a real difference in the success of the business.

After he received the offer, he went back to the *Career Priority Self-Inventory* and assessed his priorities against the priorities of the company and decided that the match between what they were offering and what he wanted was sufficiently strong to warrant serious consideration.

The one area of trade-off was on base pay and overall increase in the compensation package. A small, start-up company cannot always pay what a larger company might pay. Tom was willing to trade off a less lucrative compensation package for a day of working from home. When he calculated commuting costs (gas, wear and tear on his car, oil, etc.), and personal costs for one day a week for 49 weeks of the year, and factored them into what his base pay and

TOM'S CAREER PRIORITY SELF-INVENTORY

	✓	Personal Rating 1–10	Potential Offer 1–10
1. Ability for me to use my skills, training, and experience.	✓	⑩	10
2. Have the flexibility to work from home once a week.	✓	⑩	10
3. Opportunity to grow professionally.	✓	⑩	10
4. Work in a family-friendly environment.	✓	⑨	9
5. Experience a fair amount of autonomy.	✓	⑨	9
6. Be able to grow with the company without relocating.	✓	⑨	8
7. Increase my base pay and an overall good-to-above-average compensation package.	✓	⑧	7
8. Have the opportunity to work on new project requirements and challenges.	✓	⑦	9

quality of life would be, he actually came out ahead. Working one day a week from home would allow him to drop his son off at day care later in the morning and pick him up earlier in the afternoon. He also felt more relaxed yet fully productive working from home.

It can be challenging to figure out the value of your personal priorities because they are subjective. Only you can assess their true significance; yet they are often the most important aspects of a decision-making process. Most people learn this the hard way. They burn out or go through a downsizing situation and then they look back and say to themselves, "If only I had given a little less at work and had put more energy in at home with my family, then maybe I wouldn't feel so depleted now." Use this opportunity to figure out what is important to you in your professional life as well as in your personal life.

Striking a balance between your professional life and your personal life is easier if you have the right working conditions and environment. It takes careful thinking and some circumspection to determine what that correct work environment looks like for you.

At times, you can find it in a large corporate environment, and in other situations you will need to look into a smaller, entrepreneurial environment where procedures are more easily changed. Regardless, do your homework about yourself so that you can define the right conditions for you. This clarity about the right environment and conditions is what will make it easier for you to negotiate about areas that you want to influence and change.

Push yourself to recognize the importance of striking a balance between your personal life and your professional life. This ranking exercise can be helpful as you think about ways to strike a balance in many areas. Maria's Story illustrates how *both* the *ranking points* and the *ultimate decision* about the offer evolve:

MARIA'S STORY

Maria, an accomplished manager, was contacted by an executive search firm recruiter. The position she was under consideration for was a top-level administrative position in a prestigious academic institution. The position description, the reporting structure, the person she would report to, and the compensation were ideal. Rapport between Maria and the key contacts at the institution was strong, and she was enticed by all the trappings of what seemed like an almost perfect arrangement. There were only two drawbacks: (1) her partner would not relocate, and (2) she could not commute due to airline schedules.

The institution was located in a rural part of the Midwest and her partner was unwilling to relocate. Without the flexibility of commuting (because of erratic airline schedules), she presented the option of consulting for them. Without that as an option, she could not see her way clear to accept the offer.

Being wooed by someone from a well-known organization can be a mind-numbing experience. With some groundedness in a base of core criteria, Maria was able to pry herself away from the draw of the package, the excitement of the opportunity, and the lure of having been so strongly courted. Had she not thought through the items that were important to her, she might have developed strong resentment against her partner and some regret at being tied down.

Life is larger and more involved than just work. Balance and productivity come out of the various roles, interactions, and commitments we have in our lives. Maria's work life represented an impressive array of accomplishments. Her personal life also represented vital achievements. Based on the *Career Priority Self-Inventory*, her core criteria were:

① Work in a family-friendly environment.

② Have the flexibility to work from home once a week.

③ Be able to grow with the company without relocating.

④ Opportunity to work in a team-oriented environment.

⑤ Opportunity to work in an entrepreneurial environment.

⑥ Have a mentor or good career coach.

Three out of the six priorities were met. Ultimately, the priorities that matched the offer did not outweigh the ones that didn't *(in this case, from a life balance viewpoint),* and Maria chose to decline the opportunity.

Whether you have worked through terms of an offer or have never negotiated, taking a fresh, hard look at your key priorities can be one of the most important steps in this process. Careful work at this stage can translate into composure, conviction, and internal fortitude when you go into an actual negotiation.

Don't shortchange yourself in this work! Clarifying what is important to you enters into *every* other part of this dynamic process of negotiation.

Outline your most important priorities. Refer to the charts on pages 4–5 and transfer the top 5 to 10 career priorities to this pad.

1. _____

2. _____

3. _____

4. _____

5. _____

6. _____

7. _____

8. _____

9. _____

10. _____

Action Items

**Check
When
Completed**

——————— Figure out what is most important to you by completing the *Career Priority Self-Inventory.*

——————— Figure out *(besides salary and benefits),* the important ingredients in a good employment situation.

——————— Weigh what you know about a real or a potential offer against what is important to you.

——————— Refer to questions in Chapter 10 for areas where you need to obtain more information *(e.g., corporate culture, bonuses).*

A winner is someone who recognizes his Godgiven talents, works his tail off to develop them into skills, and uses these skills to accomplish his goals.

LARRY BIRD
BIRD ON BASKETBALL, 1986,
READING, MA: ADDISON-WESLEY

CHAPTER **2**	*Initial Response to a Job Offer*

Agenda

- **Capturing your initial reactions.**

- **Mark's Story** *(making a decision too quickly).*

- **Warnings and requests as you monitor your reaction.**

- **Following** *A Critical Path* **for the negotiation process.**

*Try not to become a man of success but rather try to become
a man of value.*

ALBERT EINSTEIN
LIFE, MAY 2, 1955

Date: Today

To: Anyone Who Receives a Job Offer

Subject: Now the Hard Part Begins — Steps to Manage Your
            Response Thoughtfully and Thoroughly

YOUR INITIAL RESPONSE TO A JOB OFFER

☺   When the thought pops into your head—Wow! I got a job offer.

☺!! Adrenaline rush!

☺? Whew, it's an offer in hand. Now, what does it mean?

☹   The offer was verbal. *Do I need to get it in writing? Ugh-oh, now
    what?* I guess I should look at the details and terms of the
    offer . . . . I don't agree with everything in the offer . . . . *What
    should I do?* I feel nervous about the thought of negotiat-
    ing . . . . *How do I need to think about this?*

Let's face it—a job search is stressful! By the time the offer comes in,
you are probably ready to close the deal quickly, but guard against a
quick decision, whether your reaction is positive or negative.

Changing jobs, weathering a transition, can be exciting and adven-
turesome, but it can also cause uneasiness. After all, you are not dealing
with something outside yourself such as a product or service. You are
dealing with *you* and your career. A job change is very personal; it is
subjective and it can be challenging. Do yourself a favor and give yourself time to think through each part of this process.

First, remember that emotions are charged during the first hours and
days after you receive an offer. Most people, if the offer is close to what
they thought would come through, probably feel good. Depending on
the way the job change has occurred, they might feel good, but also relieved. If there is an immediate reaction to the offer and that reaction
is an acceptance, the *Watch Out* is that this feeling of relief might over-
shadow some aspects of the offer that need to be more carefully explored and evaluated. Take your time before you react to the offer. You

will need that time to think clearly and logically, as Mark's Story demonstrates:

Mark's Story

Mark, a recently displaced information systems (IS) professional, explored several opportunities. The demand for highly skilled local area network (LAN) administrators was in his favor. He had numerous interviews and was very encouraged by the positive reactions to his background. The response from employers helped him overcome his negative feelings about the layoff and regain his self-esteem. He had the normal sense of loss and anger about having been forced to leave a company that he had liked. He wondered about how marketable his skills would be, and he was concerned about how well he would adjust to a new company. He also missed the companionship of his colleagues.

Mark's job search helped to alleviate his doubts about himself and about his professional worth. Within a few weeks, Mark found himself in the enviable position of receiving two job offers. One offer represented a good match between his skills and the needs of the job. It represented growth and professional development. It also seemed to represent a good match between his work style and personality and the corporate culture. It was within 20 minutes from his front door and the salary and benefits far exceeded his previous salary.

The second offer represented a good match between Mark's skills and the needs of the job, but he would have over an hour-long commute each way and the salary was lower than he wanted.

Understandably, Mark was extremely happy with the first offer. He could not believe how well suited he was for the opportunity. Within a couple of days, he accepted the offer and with anticipation, looked forward to a new set of challenges.

After Mark had been on the job for two weeks, he was overwhelmed by his responsibilities and realized that, in his hurry to take the job and his relief at not having to continue his job search, he had failed to ask specific questions about what was expected of him.

Things kept getting worse and finally, in frustration, he tried to reopen negotiations with the second company—but it was too late. He had already closed the door to that opportunity when he told them that he had found a better one.

WHAT WENT WRONG?

As Mark's experience suggests, if you do not analyze your reactions, you might act too quickly. Here is how the dynamics of the *"offer rush"* might play out:

If You Feel Tired and Relieved . . .	Watch Out Because . . .
You will want to *quickly* get on with the agreement.	You might overlook important details about the offer.
You might be fatigued and won't want to risk losing the offer.	You might *sell* yourself short.

Warnings and Requests

① *Stop* before you give your final response to an offer.

② *Think* about each detail involved in the situation and develop a thorough understanding of what will be expected of you. If you are less than 50 percent sure that you will be able to meet the expectation, *discuss* your concerns with the person to whom you will report *before* you accept the offer.

③ If all the terms of the offer appear to be good, *rigorously assess* your understanding of those terms and check your understanding with the person who has tendered the offer.

④ *Do not assume anything. Ask questions* about the offer. *Check* your assumptions about the offer. We all have assumptions and frequently we are not aware of them. Emotions cloud our thinking, and when we are excited about the positive outcome of a decision-making process, we might not be grounded in what the reality of the situation might be.

It is important to be as careful with a negative reaction to a job offer as with a positive reaction. You will usually not be able to determine whether the aspects of the offer you disagree with are subject to change. Before you turn an offer down, isolate the specific terms you do not find acceptable and formulate questions for the employer. Chapters 7 and 20 provide in-depth discussion of when not to negotiate and how to graciously decline an offer. It is difficult to sort through negative reactions. It seems easier to avoid a potential conflict than to risk a confrontation.

THE OFFER IN HAND: HOW DOES IT STACK UP?

Practical steps that are important—the *real* things that matter to me, or *"What do I want and why?"*

If you are going to look at the possibility of negotiation, do yourself a favor and start by identifying what's important to you. Some things to think about are:

The Job

- Describe the type of job you want.
- Describe the responsibilities.
- Describe the growth opportunities.

The Setting

- What kind of reporting relationship would you like?
- What level of responsibility would you like?
- Describe the culture of the organization.

Future Growth

- What might I want to progress to?
- What professional development or support might I need in order to grow?
- What opportunities are there for exposure to functions outside of mine?

Now you are prepared to focus on the following questions before you enter into a negotiation discussion. Use *A Critical Path for the Negotiation Process* as a practical road map to guide your thoughts.

Progress through the questions and proceed with calculated effort. Above all else, avoid a knee-jerk reaction to the offer.

A CRITICAL PATH FOR THE NEGOTIATION PROCESS

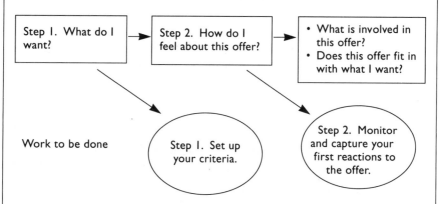

Question 1	Do the terms of the offer coincide with what is important to me in my next professional position?
Focus	• Concentrate on the position; the importance of the job in the department, division, or company; the match between your skills and the responsibilities of the job.

Question 2	What do I like about this offer?
Focus	• Is the offer fair? • How does this package compare with what I currently have?

Question 3	What do I like about this company?
Focus	• Is this a company I can grow with? • What do people in this organization value? • How have people in the position they are offering me progressed within the organization?

Question 4	Is this offer right for me?
Focus	• Is the timing right for me?

Action Items

**Check
When
Completed**

_____ Monitor your initial reactions to the offer.

_____ Review the terms of the offer with a friend or
trusted colleague.

_____ Then discuss your reactions to the offer.

_____ Follow the four steps in the "Warnings and
Requests" section of the chapter.

_____ Evaluate the offer against the three categories
of questions: The Job, The Setting, and Future
Growth.

_____ Answer the four questions listed at the end of
the chapter.

_____ Celebrate getting the offer!

*One ship drives east and the other drives west
With the selfsame winds that blow.
'Tis the set of the sails and not the gales
Which tells us the way to go.*

ELLA WHEELER WILCOX
"WINDS OF FATE"

Analyzing the Conditions and Terms of the Job Offer

Agenda

- Determine how the employer arrived at the offer *(answer questions)*.

- Identify the important internal factors that influenced the makeup of the offer.

- Understand how they arrived at the final salary.

- Identify how long the position has been open and whether people who occupied the position were promoted or not.

- Understand the value of the position in the department and the company.

- Evelyn's Story *(probing beneath the surface)*.

There is no free lunch.

MILTON FRIEDMAN

Date: Today

To: Anyone Who Reaches the Finish Line

Subject: How to Size Up a Job Offer Using the Right Tools and Measurements

---

An employer who achieves the necessary comfort level about a candidate to extend a formal invitation to join that organization still has a great deal of work ahead. Important steps for the employer include constructing an enticing offer that a candidate is likely to accept, attending to internal equity issues, inviting the candidate to accept the offer, and making it possible for the person to join the team and assimilate.

These are difficult tasks. Although a hiring representative from a company may be accustomed to extending job offers, a single hiring authority may not have the time to customize every step in the negotiation process for every candidate. Therefore, it is all the more critical that *you* delve into every aspect of the offer to assess its viability and attractiveness to *you*.

Many factors go into the composition of an offer. Dissecting the offer and understanding the details are essential to your proactive management of the negotiation process. Consider the following questions as you analyze the pieces of the offer:

How has the employer arrived at this offer?

Offer Analysis

- Was there a stated compensation range for this position?
  Your comments: _____

  _____

  _____

- Do you understand where your experience and credentials fit within such a preset range?
  Your comments: _____

  _____

  _____

- Do you have a context for understanding how your background and credentials stack up against others already at the company who hold similar positions *(especially within the same department or division—parity issues)?*
  Your comments: _____
  _____
  _____

- Has the employer articulated such factors as how much room there is to grow within a grade or "band," something which may have been figured into the offer?
  Your comments: _____
  _____
  _____

- To what extent was the offer *(at least the salary part)* based on a simple calculation (e.g., an incremental increase over your current earnings), even if you are undervalued for the market in your current position or industry?
  Your comments: _____
  _____
  _____

- Has the offer been clearly tied to stated, measurable performance objectives, especially if there is an incentive piece to the compensation *(e.g., billable hours, revenue generation, new business, cost savings)?*
  Your comments: _____
  _____
  _____

Which internal factors played a part in the makeup of this offer?

Offer Analysis

- Was it clear to everyone that this position needed to be filled?
  Your comments: _____
  _____
  _____

- What is the value of this position to the rest of the department and to the company?
  Your comments: _____

  _____

  _____

- Is there a lot of interdepartmental teamwork?
  Your comments: _____

  _____

  _____

- Is the work of the department highly valued by senior management in constructive and positive ways?
  Your comments: _____

  _____

  _____

- How is the value of the work represented?
  Your comments: _____

  _____

  _____

- Does the person occupying this position sit on important committees?
  Your comments: _____

  _____

  _____

What were the determining factors in the final salary figure?

Offer Analysis

- What role did the Human Resources Department play in setting the salary?
  Your comments: _____

  _____

  _____

- Are they expecting me to negotiate?

   Your comments: _____

   _____

   _____

How long has this position been available?

Offer Analysis

- Were any special circumstances involved in the advertisement and hiring for this job?

   Your comments: _____

   _____

   _____

- Has there been a hiring freeze? If so, what impact did that have on the department, division, or the company?

   Your comments: _____

   _____

   _____

What is the history of this job?

Offer Analysis

- Is this a new position?

   Your comments: _____

   _____

   _____

- What is the value placed on this role in the department, division, or company?

   Your comments: _____

   _____

   _____

- What important results have come from this position?
  Your comments: ⸻

  ⸻

  ⸻

Which employees in this company have held this position?

Offer Analysis

- Have they had a background similar to mine?
  Your comments: ⸻

  ⸻

  ⸻

What were their qualifications?

Offer Analysis

- Had they been promoted into the position?
  Your comments: ⸻

  ⸻

  ⸻

- Did they have specialized credentials?
  Your comments: ⸻

  ⸻

  ⸻

- Had they worked elsewhere in the company?
  Your comments: ⸻

  ⸻

  ⸻

- How long did they hold the position?
  Your comments: ⸻

  ⸻

  ⸻

Were the employees who were in this position promoted?

Offer Analysis

- If they performed well and contributed in major ways, how were they rewarded?

  Your comments: _____

  _____

  _____

- Did they receive recognition or a salary increase?

  Your comments: _____

  _____

  _____

    Use the chart on pages 27 and 31 to ① evaluate the offer against the anticipated obstacles and challenges involved in handling the areas of responsibility, then ② list your skills and strengths that will enable you to handle the specific responsibilities and challenges and, finally, ③ appraise the offer against the level of challenge and responsibility you will be expected to handle. If you find that you have gaps in information about the job, develop good questions that will get to the information you need. Chapter 10 includes questions and phrases that will help you.

    What may appear to be true on the surface, might not be. Use the chart and the questions to probe the conditions surrounding the position and the terms involved in the offer. Evelyn's Story illustrates just how much this kind of thorough probing can pay off:

EVELYN'S STORY

Evelyn, an employee communications professional, was contacted by a recruiter to interview for what she considered her dream position at her ideal company. Because she had already interacted professionally with several individuals at this company, she knew firsthand that the quality story professed by the company was accurate and that the environment would be a good fit for her personally.

    Evelyn also understood that although the specific position for which she was interviewing would use many of her existing skills, it would also require

PIECING TOGETHER AND APPRAISING THE OFFER

Outline of the Offer (1)	Anticipated Obstacles/ Challenges (2)	Outline Your Skills and Strengths (3)	Appraise the Offer (4)
• Location: _____ _____ • Title: _____ _____ • Reporting Relationship(s): _____ _____ • Responsibilities: _____ _____	Indicate whether the obstacles/ challenges might involve: limited resources, resistance from people, adverse external conditions *(competition).*	For each area of responsibility, list a strength or skill that will enable you to address the area of responsibility and challenge or obstacle associated with the responsibility.	For each area of responsibility and the accompanying degree of challenge, determine to the best of your ability how fair or appropriate the offer is. Use the offer. Use the following measurements: • *Is the base compensation fair?* • *Will the incentives (bonuses or rewards) be in line with the amount of responsibility?*
(Example)			
Start-up of a new service.	Problem with employee attitudes ⟹ they are resistant to change and market forces are not in our favor ⟹ fierce competition.	Strong project leadership, team-building, organization, and strategic planning skills.	Compensation is fair. Bonuses are fine and the available support is appropriate for the level of challenge involved.

a fair-to-moderate learning curve for the first six months to one year. Even before a formal offer was extended, the employer told her that the base salary would be lateral with what she was earning at her present company. Complicating the situation was that Evelyn received an annual increase from her current employer. During the interview process, she told the recruiter that she would entertain a lateral move—if it factored in the raise she was about to receive.

Again, before an offer from the new company was finalized, the employer told Evelyn through the recruiter that because of internal equity issues the company could not, in good faith, add on the raise she had just received. In other words, Evelyn would actually take a small cut in base salary if she joined the new company.

From the employer's perspective, Evelyn's short-term loss would be more than offset by an annual company bonus program, something her current employer did not offer, and a generous profit-sharing program for which she would become eligible in her first year of service. Most importantly, the company believed that, based on Evelyn's track record and outstanding work ethic, she would advance quickly in the organization while receiving ongoing coaching from her managers.

Evelyn saw that everything the new employer was saying had validity. Not only was there no bonus or profit-sharing program at her current organization, but she was also "topped out," no mentoring was available to help her expand her skill base. Evaluating the current opportunity versus the new opportunity, made Evelyn's decision fairly easy. Her thought process went something like this:

Current Employer	New Employer
• No room for growth—organization not growing.	• Lots of room for growth—growing organization in exploding industry.
• No formal or informal mentoring available.	• Several role models and coaches to provide constant mentoring.
• Annual merit increases steady, but no larger incentives that reward performance.	• Steady annual merit increases plus exceptional company incentive package.
• Not enough professional and intellectual stimulation.	• An environment buzzing with excitement and bright, interesting colleagues.

Looking at these scenarios side by side, Evelyn was prepared to take the short-term base cut and join the new organization. The long-term potential outweighed what she now perceived as a relatively short-term concession. However, there was another significant wrinkle; during the interview process, a second outside organization began to court Evelyn.

The second organization, a prestigious management consulting firm, offered excellent opportunities for advancement in a rapidly growing industry. It also offered mentoring and a pay-for-performance incentive program. And, it was prepared to offer Evelyn a 20 percent base increase over her current salary.

Now the decision process had a third layer. Evelyn already had determined that she would leave her current organization. But now she had to decide between two outside offers.

At first glance, the 20 percent increase seemed hard to refuse. After all, it had many of the pluses, at least superficially, that attracted her to the first outside position, and the initial compensation package was very seductive. But Evelyn made herself focus, and she probed more deeply. Having eliminated her current employer from consideration, here is what her thought process looked like now:

New Organization 1	New Organization 2
• Plenty of opportunities for growth and mentoring.	• Plenty of opportunities for growth and mentoring.
• Large, well-regarded organization in high-growth industry.	• Large, well-regarded organization in high-growth industry.
• Positive work environment with a value system that encouraged having a life outside the job (*reflected in reasonable work hours, not 9-to-5, but average of 45–50 hours per week*).	• Very strenuous work environment with a tacit understanding that there would be some 60- to 80-hour work weeks, especially during peak times of the year.
• Excellent long-term total compensation package (*reflected in ongoing profit-sharing program that acknowledges tenure as well as position level*).	• Long-term compensation closely tied to whether or not you become eligible for a senior level position in the organization.
• Low turnover rate—employees seem happy and challenged—not burned out.	• Moderate-to-high turnover rate—employees are stimulated but some look exhausted.
• Stay in suburbs—no commute to a major city.	• Commute to a major city required, along with additional 5 percent city wage tax deducted from pay.
• Initial pay cut; even though the raise at current job had just come through, there is still some concern about taking a step back.	• 20 percent base salary increase is somewhat offset by wage tax, commuting time, and longer hours required overall.

When Evelyn looked at all the factors, she decided to join Organization 1. By thinking through all the variables, she saw that the large immediate pay increase came with some serious disadvantages. When she looked beneath the surface of the enticing salary, she saw that things like a balanced life and an environment where she could pace herself and move steadily ahead without burning out were extremely important to her. There seemed to be a better match between her own core values and those of the first employer.

Just one month into her new job, Evelyn is already very happy with her choice, and her new employer is delighted with her enthusiasm and early performance.

The moral of the story: *Don't be surprised by surprises!* Sometimes the things you think you want the most when entering a negotiation (in this case, a larger salary) turn out not to be the deciding variables.

The commitment you make to a new employer is significant. With close scrutiny of the inner dynamics of the position, you can avoid some of the pitfalls. For those of you concerned about over-analyzing the details of the offer, remember to take it one step at a time. Spend enough time to investigate the behind-the-scenes aspects of the offer *so that you command more of the process.*

You will need to stay somewhat organized so that you can ask the right questions at the right time. Use the chart *Piecing Together and Appraising the Offer* on page 31 to strategically evaluate the offer. Then turn to the memo board on page 32 for important questions designed to give you a thorough understanding of the offer.

PIECING TOGETHER AND APPRAISING THE OFFER

Outline of the Offer	Anticipated Obstacles and Challenges	Outline Your Skills	Appraise the Offer
Location			
Title			
Reporting Relationship(s)			
Responsibilities			

Conditions and Terms of the Offer Notebook

Important Questions   **Answers**

• How did you arrive at the offer? _____
  _____

• Did internal factors play a role? _____
  _____

• What factors influenced the level of compensation? _____
  _____

• What type of support exists for this position? _____
  _____

• What in your opinion are the more significant challenges in the
  position? Why? _____
  _____

• How would you define success in this position and why? ____
  _____

• In what ways are incentives, salary, and recognition factored
  into the offer package? _____
  _____

• What do you value most about the experience I would bring to
  this position? _____
  _____

• Please describe possible growth in the company. _____
  _____
  _____

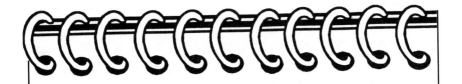

Action Items

_____ Work through questions about the offer and the internal conditions surrounding the offer.

_____ Study Evelyn's Story and use it to check your assumptions about how you might respond to an offer.

_____ Work through the chart entitled *Piecing Together and Appraising the Offer.*

_____ Use the *Conditions and Terms of the Offer Notebook* to organize the questions most important to you and targeted dates for getting answers.

Other follow up steps I will take:

_____

_____

_____

_____

_____

_____

I'll make him an offer he can't refuse.

MARIO PUZO, 1920–
AMERICAN NOVELIST,
THE GODFATHER, 1969, CHAPTER 1

CHAPTER 4	*Assessing the Conditions and Terms of the Offer against Your Core Selection Criteria*

Agenda

- Figure out how well the offer fits your criteria.

- Assess what is acceptable about the offer.

- Ann's Story *(standing firm on your core criteria)*.

- Consider your priorities and look for trade-offs.

- Work through the *Personal Assessment Worksheet*.

You have succeeded in life when all you really want is only what you really want.

VERNON HOWARD

Date: Today

To: Those Who Want to Know How to Assess the Conditions and Terms of the Offer *against* Your Core Selection Criteria

Subject: Steps to Master the Assessment Process

A WAY TO THINK ABOUT THIS: THREE IMPORTANT QUESTIONS

① *What do I know about the offer?*

② *What must I have (inflexible criteria)?*

③ *What do I want that can possibly be negotiated (nice to have, but more flexible criteria)?*

Details about a job offer can cloud your thinking if you find that the details don't agree with what you want. *If you have yet to zero in on your core priorities and criteria, go back to Chapter 1 to complete the exercise and read the cases (Tom's Story; Maria's Story).* The work in Chapter 1 will help you gain control over this process. If you are clear about your priorities and core selection criteria, you will be more centered and able to calibrate terms of the job offer against something valid and stable. If your approach to the offer is void of in-depth self-evaluation, you will probably find yourself swayed by aspects of the offer that might have short-lived meaning and value. The following case exemplifies what often happens:

ANN'S STORY

Ann received a seductive offer from a prominent financial services company after much back-and-forth discussion on issues like a sign-on bonus and relocation expenses. The discussions about the bonus and the relocation were intense—the candidate needed to be assured that she would not lose money in the move, especially since she would be forfeiting a forthcoming bonus from her current employer. But, the employer and the candidate enjoyed an excellent rapport and these issues were resolved quite amicably. The candidate was ready to accept.

There was only one hitch—the position itself did not meet a major, if not **the** major, core criterion: expanding her marketing expertise beyond the financial services industry! She reevaluated and subsequently declined the offer with much disappointment all around. Psychologically, both the candidate and the employer were ready to work together. But, in getting caught up in negotiating over key compensation points, she had lost sight of one of her main stated goals for changing jobs in the first place.

It is easy to see how not keeping *all* your core criteria in front of you can get you sidetracked.

Taking the following steps will facilitate increased clarity and will minimize confusion. Break the assessment process down into the following eight steps:

Step 1   *Review* the items that you have decided are important to you. Use the *Career Priority Self-Inventory* in Chapter 1.

Step 2   *Talk* with others who have a background similar to yours to make certain that you are including *all* major points.

Step 3   *Collect* all your notes about the job and the organization. If you are sure that you have complete information, go to *Step 4*. If not, get answers to your remaining questions and then proceed to *Step 4*.

Step 4   *Combine* information about the conditions and terms of the offer with answers to the following questions on pages 37–38.

Step 5   *Capture* the information about the terms and conditions of the offer *and* the core criteria on the *Personal Assessment Worksheet* and determine where a match exists and where it does not exist.

Step 6   *Identify* aspects of the offer in question.

Step 7   *Decide* what you might want to negotiate about.

Step 8   *Identify* issues you might have that will require special planning and which you will need to address (see the Sample Offer letter on p. 39).

PERSONAL ASSESSMENT WORKSHEET

Conditions/ Terms of the Offer	Your Core Criteria	Is There a Fit?		
		Yes	No	Maybe (To Be Negotiated)
Job Responsibilities	• What do I want in my next job?	____	____	____
	• What kinds of responsibilities do I want to address?	____	____	____
Reporting	• What kind of reporting relationship do I want?	____	____	____
	• How would I describe the ideal reporting relationship?	____	____	____
Travel	• How much travel will be involved in the position and how does this fit in with what I prefer?	____	____	____
	• If there is travel over 25% of the time, do the trips, on average, involve one night or more than one night?	____	____	____
	• What amount of the travel is domestic?	____	____	____
	• What amount of the travel is international?	____	____	____
Balance	• How do I define balance between my work life and my personal life?	____	____	____
	• What do I need to create this balance?	____	____	____
	• Will this position help me create this kind of balance?	____	____	____
Culture	• In what kind of corporate culture do I do my best work? Why?	____	____	____
	• How does the culture of this organization fit in with my description of an ideal culture?	____	____	____

(continued)

Personal Assessment Worksheet (continued)

Conditions/ Terms of the Offer	Your Core Criteria	Is There a Fit? Yes	No	Maybe (To Be Negotiated)
Relocation	• Does the position require relocation?	____	____	____
	• How often am I willing to relocate?	____	____	____
Geographic Preference	• How important is this geographic region to me?	____	____	____
	• Why is this region important?	____	____	____
	• What other geographic preferences do I have?	____	____	____
	• Whom do I need to take into consideration when considering geographic preferences?	____	____	____
Compensation	• How much do I need to earn?	____	____	____
	• How willing am I to be flexible with the amount that I earn?	____	____	____
Benefits	• What do I need to have for:			
	Medical coverage?	____	____	____
	Insurance?	____	____	____
	Pension?	____	____	____
	Rental coverage?	____	____	____
	Child care?	____	____	____
	Tuition reimbursement?	____	____	____
	Vacation?	____	____	____
	Personal leave?	____	____	____
Performance Review	• What do I want to get out of a performance review?	____	____	____
	• Is part of my compensation tied to the performance rating?	____	____	____

SAMPLE OFFER LETTER

Dear Margaret:

We are pleased to extend an offer of employment to you. Your primary areas of responsibility will include:

- Business forecasting for X Brand in the North American market.
- Leading an 8-member team of analysts.
- Presenting weekly trend reports to the Vice President of Sales and her team.
- Leading a cross-functional task force for Initiatives, Product Development, and Marketing for your Brand.

You will represent your Brand in all senior level meetings and will be expected to provide comprehensive information about the strategic positioning of the Brand in your sector of the market.

Ask about

Your compensation will include a bonus *(which will be based on an industry standard formula)* for reaching targeted sales goals for your Brand.

Your performance will be reviewed on a semiannual basis. Categories for the review will include:

Ask for examples & historical pattern of success

1/3: Demonstrated leadership in your primary, secondary, and tertiary teams.

1/3: Leadership in providing accurate data for strategic planning for your Brand.

1/3: Tactical mobilization of new *initiatives* for your Brand in the marketplace and for reaching stretch goals on time and within budget.

Ask about amount of travel & precedents for regional & national leadership

You will be expected to represent your teams at regional and national trade shows and to assume prominent stature within the appropriate national associations.

Your compensation package includes:

- $160,000 per annum.
- Bonus *(as outlined in paragraph 3)*.
- Profit sharing *(description of the corporate profit sharing plan is attached)*.
- Benefits *(cafeteria-style benefits plan enclosed)*.
- Pension plan *(description enclosed)*.

We look forward to having you on our team beginning May 15. We are impressed with your track record and look forward to a successful joining of talent.

Please don't hesitate to call me if you have any questions.

Sincerely,

Brenda Beatty

Take the 8 steps and, for a final quality check, make sure that you have answered the three questions we started with:

① *What do I know about the offer?* (Do I know enough or do I need to go back to the employer?)

② *What must I have* (no flexibility with these criteria)?

③ *What do I want that can possibly be negotiated* (nice to have, but more flexible criteria)?

Delve into the exercises in Chapters 8–10, 16, and 18–19 if you anticipate any difficulty in negotiating aspects of the offer.

Action Items

**Check
When
Completed**

_____ Go to Chapter 1 to review your career priorities and criteria.

_____ Go to Chapter 3 to review your appraisal of the job offer.

_____ Identify areas of trade-off among your career priorities.

_____ Complete the *Personal Assessment Worksheet* and zero in on items you might want to bring up in a negotiation.

The secret of success is constancy of purpose.

BENJAMIN DISRAELI
SPEECH AT BANQUET OF NATIONAL UNION OF
CONSERVATIVE AND CONSTITUTIONAL ASSOCIATIONS,
CRYSTAL PALACE, LONDON, JUNE 24, 1872

Understanding the Needs, Goals, and Perspectives of the Employer

Agenda

• The biggest pitfall for negotiators.

• Martin's Story *(the consequences of not learning enough about a prospective employer)*.

• Questions to help you ascertain the employer's needs and pressures.

• Questions to help you understand the employer's perspective.

• Three common hurdles to scale when trying to understand the employer's needs, goals, and perspectives.

Only the educated are free.

EPICTETUS

Date: Today

To: Those of You Trying to Understand the *Needs, Goals,* and *Perspectives* of the Employer

Subject: The Three Categories You Need to Get Clear On

Among the biggest pitfalls for most people is the need to gain a clear, comprehensive understanding of the employer's side. They run into a win-lose scenario and fail to get what they want. Avoid this common error. Consider the following hard lesson learned:

MARTIN'S STORY

Martin was a finance professional who had decided to lay the groundwork for transitioning out of his company before a pending restructuring. Not knowing what the outcome of the reorganization would be like, he felt more in charge of his career by putting his resume out in the marketplace. Although he had not done this in several years and felt a little unprepared for the job search process, he had a good resume and had kept in contact with people in his profession through his work in a professional association. He also had a good reputation as a manager.

It took Martin several months of circulating his resume to secure interviews. Finally, he found what seemed to be a good fit. The opportunity was in his field and would allow him to stretch. The company had a good reputation and strong presence in the market, and he would not have to relocate to another region of the country.

Martin was called in for three interviews and felt certain that not only was he their top candidate, but that he could make a difference in their company. After the third interview, the hiring manager called Martin to let him know that they were going to tender an offer of employment. Martin was eager to receive the offer letter.

On receipt, he reviewed the terms of the offer and was surprised to find the base salary was lower than he had assumed it would be and his title would not be as prestigious as his former title.

Admitting to some naiveté (because he had never been faced with this situation before) and bravado (because he felt caught off guard and insulted by the pay), he called the employer. With some controlled frustration present in his voice, he asked for a meeting to discuss the offer. The dialogue went like this:

Martin: Hi, Barbara. I received your letter. Could I come in so that we can talk about the details of the offer?

Barbara: Yes. We look forward to having you on board. I have some time tomorrow between 2:30 and 4:00. Do you want to come in then?

Martin: Yes, that will work. Thank you.

Barbara: Martin, before we hang up, is the offer in line with what you have been looking for or are there some major problems with it?

Martin: Barbara, there are several aspects of the offer that work, but I have serious reservations about the salary and the title.

Barbara: Oh, I see. I thought we shared our policy of handling all new employees in a similar manner. Everyone starts at this rate, and we are a flat organization, so we all carry that title when we start here. That is part of our culture.

Martin: It would be better to talk about this in person. If that's all right with you, let's discuss this tomorrow at 2:30.

Barbara: That's fine. I'll look forward to seeing you.

When Martin and Barbara met, they were primed to defend their respective positions. The positive momentum that had led to the offer fell victim to Martin's insistence that the salary be significantly increased and to Barbara's insistence that they as a company could not budge on the salary level nor on the title. Martin did not take the job and felt somewhat defeated, and Barbara felt that Martin was arrogant and that she probably would not have liked working with him.

During the interviews, *how could Martin have avoided this outcome?* He could have probed for the following information:

- Please describe your organization. Is it flat or highly structured? How are titles determined?

- Please describe the typical person who joins the firm.

- What do you emphasize as you bring new employees into the organization?

- As I anticipate moving from my current employer to your organization, what might I expect?

Martin's story demonstrates why it is critical to delve into the motivations and needs of the employer. Isn't representing yourself good enough? *No. The process of attempting to understand the employer would have given Martin a realistic picture. The more data you have, the more alternatives you will be able to generate. The more alternatives you have, the greater will be your chance for success.* If Martin had been aware of the company's culture, he probably would have discontinued the process earlier on and would have felt better about himself and the process.

How can *you* understand the needs, goals, and perspectives of the employer when you have your own concerns to pay attention to, and you are putting effort into representing yourself well? *It takes well-thought-out questions and method. Try to prevent operating out of a false sense of confidence.*

Consider the following dimensions of the *Employer's Pressures/Needs, Goals for the Position, and Perspective* as you work on developing a better understanding of the employer.

EMPLOYER'S PRESSURES/NEEDS, GOALS FOR THE POSITION, AND PERSPECTIVE

Pressures/Needs

① What pressure is the employer under to fill this position?

② If pressure exists, why does it? *(Where does it come from?)*

③ How is the company performing?

④ Is the company, division, or department facing difficulties?

⑤ How would you describe the organizational climate?

⑥ Are they appropriately staffed for the objectives they want to achieve?

⑦ Are they financially secure?

⑧ What are the challenges they face *(e.g., internal politics or strife, market presence and competition, staffing, resources)?*

Goals for the Position

① How important is this position in the department, division, and company?

② Why is it important?

③ What are the politics associated with this position and this functional area?

④ How has the employer assessed my potential contributions to the position and organization?

    a. What do they need that I can help them with?

    b. What motivated them to make the offer to me?

⑤ How many people have they offered the job to?

⑥ Are their *expectations* of me *reasonable?*

⑦ How have people performed in this position in the past?

⑧ What has contributed to their success?

⑨ What has existed as an impediment or barrier to good performance?

⑩ Are there any unusual or unique circumstances involved in this position and in the company?

Perspective

① What role might I play in the success of the organization?

② What is most important to this employer and to the person with whom I have been dealing?

③ Has the person with whom I have been dealing had experience in the hiring and negotiation process?

④ How might this person approach a negotiation?

    a. Will he or she have the authority to decide on changes in the terms of the offer? *(Does someone else need to be brought into the meeting to best facilitate the decision-making process?)*

    b. Might the employer be offended by my response to the offer?

    c. Is the person with whom I am dealing accustomed to negotiation?

    d. What can I do to reinforce the positive aspects of our relationship? *(Is there anything I need to be sensitive to as I begin to talk with the employer? Are there pressures that the company is under or is there a perception that the offer is competitive and does not warrant further discussion?)*

    e. Do I need to do any more research before I approach them?

It is important to put yourself in the employer's shoes. Only when you probe for the important priorities of the other person and of the organization can you step into the other half of the equation that makes up a workable negotiation process. It is natural to overlook this part of the process. It is hard enough to be clear and comprehensive about your own priorities. Trying to traverse the territory of the "other" party *(the employer)* can feel foreign and uncomfortable.

Some hurdles you might encounter as you address the questions are:

Hurdle 1. You don't have enough information to answer most of the questions.

Response: Design nonthreatening, open-ended questions that you can ask the employer. You need to ask these *before* you try to discuss terms of the offer *(see Chapter 10 when you develop your questions).*

For example, for the first question under *Pressures/Needs,* "What pressure is the employer under to fill this position?" your questions could be:

- In what ways would you describe the role this position plays in the division and in the organization?
- In what ways do other people in the organization depend on this role for information, support, guidance, and leadership?
- In what ways has this vacancy affected the business?

Hurdle 2. Gathering more information from the employer in a timely fashion could be difficult given how busy everyone is.

Response:

- Plan to use e-mail and faxes, as well as short *(15–20 minutes)* exchanges over the telephone, to get your questions answered.
- When you have in-person or telephone meetings, send the company's representative(s) your questions before the meeting to make your time together as substantive as possible.
- Expect to have several meetings with the employer. At each meeting, while you are learning about the areas in question, you will gain information about their culture, the climate in which they

conduct business, the pace of activity, and the people who work at the organization.

Hurdle 3. You might be dealing with inexperienced representatives from the company.

Response: Anticipate how you can assist them in their job as you work through the negotiation process. If they might feel uncomfortable in representing the organization and engaging in what might feel like a confrontational exchange, *start the discussion with strong positive statements about the way they have treated you in past interactions.*

- Validate the relationship and thank them for the offer, *for example, I have felt very comfortable here and welcome the opportunity to work here. I thank you for the offer.*

- Ask them about what is most important to them: *I would like to know more about your priorities. I would like to be of support to you. Could you describe your top priorities and why they are important to you?*

- Establish a common focus on looking for areas of flexibility: *As we discuss a few gaps between the structure of the offer and my goals in my next professional move, can we examine areas that lend themselves to flexibility?*

Devote time and effort to stepping away from your needs and concerns so that you can appreciate the needs, goals, and perspectives of the employer. Negotiating involves relating. The more effectively you are able to relate to the motivations, pressures, and priorities of the employer, the more you can tailor your issues to their frame of reference. Try to fit your concerns into their perspective—I guarantee that you will be more successful in your negotiation process.

Action Items

**Check
When
Completed**

_____ Anticipate and answer questions about the employer's needs.

_____ Review Martin's Story and notice where you might identify.

_____ Refer to Chapter 5 for examples of open-ended questions.

_____ Answer questions about the employer's pressures and needs.

_____ Answer questions about the employer's goals for the position.

_____ Answer questions about the employer's perspective.

_____ Plan your responses to the three most common negotiating hurdles.

He who knows only his own side of the case knows little of that.

JOHN STUART MILL

Evaluating the Market Demand for Your Expertise

Agenda

- Getting the right information to determine your market value.
- The resources to tap into.
- Questions to ask a reference librarian.
- How to *use* a professional association.
- How to tap into alumni association resources.
- Working with a recruiter and checking out other resources.
- Questions to use when researching your market value.
- Using a "T" chart.
- Questions to ask the employer during the last interview or when you first receive a job offer.
- *Preparation Self-Critique.*

An education isn't how much you have committed to memory, or even how much you know. It's being able to differentiate between what you do know and what you don't. It's knowing where to go to find out what you need to know; and it's knowing how to use the information you get.

ATTRIBUTED TO WILLIAM FEATHER—AUGUST KORBEE
QUOTABLE QUOTES ON EDUCATION, 1968, UNVERIFIED

Date: Today

To: Market-Savvy Negotiators

Subject: How to Evaluate the Real Market Demand for
            Your Expertise

Figuring out what you are worth is one of the most important ways you can arm yourself when you enter into a negotiation.

HOW TO GET THE RIGHT INFORMATION

Anyone who has gone on a mission to find important information knows that it is critical to have a healthy sense of curiosity, determination, and a spirit of adventure. Make a commitment now to learn how to get the right information, *and* have fun in the process! Be aware of the following resources and use them expediently:

Resources

- **Public Libraries**—Reference Section

    Present some of the following questions to a *reference librarian:*

    Where can I find salary information listed by professional field?

    Where can I find a list of executive recruiters? (or Where can I find *The Directory of Executive Recruiters,* annual publication [Kennedy Publications, Fitzwilliam, NH]?)

    Where can I find cost-of-living information by geographic region of the country? (or Do you carry *The National Business Employment Weekly?*)

    Where can I find information about supply/demand for my field in this geographic region?

- **Professional Associations**—Membership Salary Surveys

    Most associations conduct salary surveys. They also have a newsletter and/or a magazine. The articles usually cover trends in the profession as well as innovative aspects of the work. Call the membership person for either the regional chapter or the national chapter and ask them for trends, supply/demand, and salary-related information. If you find an article that includes this type of data and would like more information, contact the author of the article. If you do not belong to an association, refer to the *Encyclopedia of Associations: An Associations Unlimited Reference,* 1997, Gale Research, 835 Penobscott Building, Detroit, MI 48226-4094, in the reference section of a public library. Listings of associations are organized by subject and geographic location.

- **The Alumni Association of Your Alma Mater**

  Increasingly, colleges and universities are providing some level of service to alumni who are job hunting. At a minimum, you will need to join the association, which will give you access to alumni in your area or to alumni (via E-mail or telephone) throughout the country. Offer to make a donation to the university after you secure your next job.

How to Tap into the Resources

- **Professional Recruiters** ("Headhunters")

  Read Chapter 12 and then develop your own list of questions for the recruiter. Recruiters can be an ally and a very good source of information about the market.

- **Colleagues**

  The adage "everyone knows someone" works wonders here. If you can ask your coworkers/colleagues questions about market demand *or,* better yet, ask them for the name of a good recruiter in your field—you might easily get what you are looking for. Also ask them for a relevant publication for your field.

- *The National Business Employment Weekly*

  This is a very good publication for:

  Cost-of-living information for every major region of the country.

  Salary surveys.

Articles about every topic related to job change.

Professional opportunities.

It is published by Dow Jones & Company, Inc.; for information about a local distributor or subscription fees, call (800) Job-Hunt (562–4868).

- **Chambers of Commerce**

  Your local chamber of commerce can be a good resource. The larger the business community, the stronger might be your chamber of commerce. They serve a number of functions:

  They serve as a local, regional, and statewide voice for businesses.

  They serve as a recruitment source for new businesses and are referred to as a resource for economic development.

  They encourage probusiness activities and events and sometimes have cost-of-living information and average salary information.

  They often have a Senior Corps of Retired Executives (SCORE) group serving as advisors to local businesses.

  They often have a library.

  They offer benefits to members such as networking, and discounts on cellular phone service.

  Use your local chamber if you can. The person responsible for membership might be a good place to start if you are trying to collect supply/demand or salary information.

- **The Internet**

  Begin by accessing information from a Web page for the professional associations most relevant for your profession. For addresses, e-mail, and Web page addresses refer to the *Encyclopedia of Associations* cited earlier in this chapter.

- **Department of Labor—Bureau of Labor Statistics Publications**

  The Occupational Outlook Quarterly provides profiles of specific professional areas, average salaries for the specific field, professional associations linked to each professional field, and some general supply/demand information. *The Occupational Outlook Handbook* is a larger publication that is issued less frequently. This could be useful to you but beware of outdated information.

- *Electronic Job Search Revolution,* 1996, Joyce Lain Kennedy and Thomas J. Morrow. John Wiley & Sons, Inc., New York, NY.
- *The Information Please Business Almanac Desk Reference,* Seth Godin, Editor. Houghton Mifflin Company, 215 Park Avenue South, New York, NY 10003.

Use the following questions when going to these sources:

① In the labor market at large, what is the *supply/demand* situation for my experience, credentials, and track record?

② What is *most marketable* about my background and credentials?

③ What is the *average salary* paid to most people with my background?

④ What is an *average salary range* that most people with my background fall into?

⑤ If I am transferring my skills from one industry to another, what do I need to do to promote the relevance and strength of my background? Use the following "T" chart:

What Do They Need?	What Can I Contribute? (You Fill in This Side)
• Which skills are most highly valued?	_____
• What training is most highly valued?	_____
• What type of experience is most valued?	_____

⑥ Are annual bonuses common in my field?

⑦ Are hiring bonuses common in my field?

⑧ What does the benefit package usually include? What do I have to watch out for?

⑨ If I am relocating, what is the cost of living in the area I am considering moving to?

QUESTIONS TO ASK THE EMPLOYER

Ask these questions toward the end of your interview process or when you first receive the offer:

- How many people with similar qualifications have interviewed for the position?

- What combination of experience, skill, and training have you been looking for that you have not been able to find in other candidates but that I possess?

Finally, use the following chart to gauge your approach:

PREPARATION SELF-CRITIQUE

① In what way can I best evaluate this offer and prepare for possible negotiations? _____

_____

_____

_____

② Am I being fair to myself as I appraise my value as a professional?

_____

_____

_____

③ In what ways am I possibly being:
- Short-sighted? _____
- Superficial and/or cursory? _____

- Intimidated by the process or by the employer? _____
- Naive about what I am worth in the marketplace? _____
- Too humble? _____
- Narrow minded? _____
- Too ego driven? _____
- Presumptuous about what they might or might not change?___

_____

Keep in mind that you do not know what is or is not negotiable until you do some homework—go in armed with good factual data and give the process a try.

Action Items

**Check
When
Completed**

_____ Refer to the *Resources* that will help you *answer* the question *"What is my market value."*

_____ Review questions to ask a reference librarian.

_____ Go over what to ask the employer during the final interview or when you first receive the offer.

_____ Work through the *Preparation Self-Critique.*

_____ Think about how to *use* a professional recruiter (*also* read Chapter 12).

If a man empties his purse into his head no one can take it away from him. An investment in knowledge always pays the best interest.

ATTRIBUTED TO BENJAMIN FRANKLIN
POOR RICHARD'S ALMANAC

Making the Decision: When and When Not to Negotiate

Agenda

- Make sure the position and the offer are close enough to your priorities and criteria to warrant serious consideration.

- Make sure the position is well suited for your experience and goals.

- Evaluate how and/or if you would be able to contribute something of value to the organization.

- Determine whether you could grow with the organization.

- Identify the number of items on your list of priorities important enough to engage in a negotiation.

Let us never negotiate out of fear, but let us never fear to negotiate.

JOHN F. KENNEDY
INAUGURAL ADDRESS, JANUARY 20, 1961, *THE OXFORD DICTIONARY OF MODERN QUOTATIONS*, 1991, EDITED BY TONY AUGARDE, OXFORD, ENGLAND: OXFORD UNIVERSITY PRESS

When an offer first comes through, you may experience a range of re-actions. Regardless of your circumstances *(whether you are a seasoned professional weathering restructuring unemployment, a newly minted MBA with some experience, or a recently graduated engineer or profes-sional student)*, the offer will make you feel good. Even if it is not the preferred or ideal offer, an offer is a symbolic endorsement of your value as a professional. Make sure you recognize the accomplishment an offer represents.

Professional transition and a job search can be tough on your ego and your self-esteem. Take a moment to bask in the glory of an offer of em-ployment and celebrate the milestone.

After your initial reactions, the reality sets in that the moment to ne-gotiate has finally arrived— if you *choose* to negotiate. Yes, one of your choices is *not* to negotiate!

So, how do you approach this choice point, especially if before start-ing this chapter you automatically assumed that the only logical response to a job offer is to engage in a negotiation? You need to break the surface of this assumption and *instead* engage in some tough self-analysis.

First, you must be honest with yourself about what is most important to you. Refer back to the self-critique you worked through in Chapter 1. The articulation of important criteria for professional satisfaction will serve as a navigational chart in answering the critical question *"What do I value in my professional life?"*

It is critical to become crystal clear about your professional values and priorities *before* you decide whether or not to negotiate. The prospect of negotiating catapults you into a position of refined focus about what matters most to you (just as running a race requires that you focus on the time you want to run it in and the condition you need to be in, in order to achieve your time). We take a lot for granted in most areas of our lives, and only when a special opportunity or event arises can we skillfully freeze-frame a section of our routine to evaluate our actions or decisions with heightened awareness. Receiving a viable offer can cause you to question what you value and why you value some things over others.

To examine the question *"What do I really value in my professional life?"* think about your core values as points that lie somewhere in between two opposing ends of a spectrum. The 13 (a baker's dozen!) categories of professional priorities in the following chart will give you the opportunity to do just that. To complete the *Professional Priority Spectrum,* you must evaluate each end of the spectrum *independent* of the job offer in front of you.

Where you place the "X" on each line should reflect your constant, core values, not a momentary reaction to a specific offer or circumstance.

Start with this example:

Teamwork ◄—————————————— **X** ——————► Autonomy

I placed my "X" almost all the way at the *Autonomy* end of the spectrum. Under "Comments," I would then briefly explain *why* I chose that placement: "I would rather control my workload independently than be tied in to a group effort most of the time." Using this pattern complete the following exercise:

PROFESSIONAL PRIORITY SPECTRUM

① Teamwork ◄——————————————————► Autonomy

Comments: _____

_____

② Multifunctional Responsibility ◄——————————► Specialization

Comments: _____

_____

③ Leadership ◄——————————————————► Leadership
   (Formal)   *(Functional)*

Comments: _____

_____

(The difference between *formal* and *functional* leadership is that formal leadership involves more authority across departmental lines and functional leadership is more specific to one department. A controller has broad-based accountability for compliance and policy and authority in an organization. An accountant is a leader in daily/weekly/monthly accuracy.)

④ Competitive Work ◄————————————► Collegiality and
   Environment   Cooperative Teamwork

   Comments: _____

   _____

⑤ Opportunities for ◄————————————► Professional Growth
   Promotion   and Development

   Comments: _____

   _____

⑥ Bonus/Profit Sharing ◄————————————► Excellent Fixed Benefits

   Comments: _____

   _____

⑦ Minimal Travel Required ◄————————————► Extensive Travel Required
   (less than 25%)   *(more than 40%)*

   Comments: _____

   _____

⑧ Family-Friendly Environment ◄————————► Competitive Work Environment

   Comments: _____

   _____

⑨ Established Organization ◄————————————► Entrepreneurial, Young Organization

   Comments: _____

   _____

(continued)

⑩ High-Tech Environment ◄————————► Traditional Environment
(e.g., requires fundamental knowledge of wide range of systems and software)

Comments: _____

_____

⑪ Regionally Based Organization ◄————————► Nationwide Organization

Comments: _____

_____

⑫ National Organization ◄————————► Multinational Organization

Comments: _____

_____

⑬ Open Communication ◄————————► Hierarchical Communication

Comments: _____

_____

Additional Comments: _____

_____

_____

_____

_____

ISOLATING THE IMPORTANT INFORMATION

Now take a close look at the *Professional Priority Spectrum* and identify the five priorities that are *most* important to you.

This step involves hard-core discernment. Notice where you have marked your "X's" and make sure that your feelings about each value are strong enough to sustain repeated scrutiny.

Now transfer the information from the *Professional Priority Spectrum* to the following boxes. This exercise prompts you to list five priorities, but feel free to list more.

Priority 1: _____

Why is it a priority? _____

_____

_____

_____

Priority 2: _____

Why is it a priority? _____

_____

_____

_____

Priority 3: _____

Why is it a priority? _____

_____

_____

_____

Priority 4: _____

Why is it a priority? _____

_____

_____

_____

Priority 5: _____

Why is it a priority? _____

_____

_____

_____

Offer Analysis—Part I

Now that you have completed the hardest—and potentially most confronting—part of this process, relax, take a deep breath, and pull out the job offer itself. The next part of the process will simply help you streamline and summarize some *objective* information. Complete the *Offer Analysis (Part I)*:

Offer Analysis (Part I)

What does the offer entail?

• Date of the offer: _____

• The offer was made: In person ☐   Over the phone ☐   In writing ☐

• Name of the person who made the offer: _____

• Title of the person who made the offer: _____

• Their role/responsibilities in the organization: _____

_____

• Name of the organization: _____

• Address: _____

_____

• Telephone number: _____

Fax number: _____

• Industry organization is involved with:

Primary industry: _____

Secondary industry: _____

Other: _____

• Describe the offer:

Title: _____

Functional responsibilities:

Primary: _____

Secondary: _____

Reporting relationship(s): _____

Name: _____

Title: _____

Background/years of service: _____

Work system *(team cross-functional responsibilities, hierarchical):* _____
_____

How they describe their ideal professional in this position: _____
_____

Base compensation: _____

Incentive system(s): _____

Bonus plan *(average annual percentage):* _____ %

Hiring (sign-on) bonus: Yes ☐   No ☐

If *yes,* amount: $ _____

Stock options: _____

Profit sharing: _____

- Benefits:
  Healthcare: Provider(s): _____

  Insurance: Copay: _____

  Cost for individual: _____

  Cost for family: _____

  Describe coverage: _____
  _____

Dental: Provider(s): _____

                  Insurance: Copay: _____

Short-term disability: Terms: _____

Long-term disability: Terms: _____

- Pension Plan: Terms: _____

                  _____

           Life Insurance: _____

           Tuition Reimbursement: _____

- Vacation:

           Number of weeks: _____

           Effective when: _____

- Number of sick days: _____

- Number of personal leave days: _____

- Performance Review:

System: _____

When performance review is conducted: _____

By whom: _____

- Start date: _____

- Orientation/Introductions (please check the ways in which you will be intro-
duced to your new colleagues):

    ☐ Meetings _____

    ☐ Newsletter _____

    ☐ One-to-One Meetings _____

    ☐ E-mail _____

- Names and titles of close working associates: _____

_____

_____

OFFER ANALYSIS (PART II)

After laying out the objective parameters of the offer, it is time to dig a little deeper. Now consider the more *subjective* aspects of the offer. Full assessment of these items probably has involved—or still needs to involve—direct dialogue with the employer. Complete Part II to the best of your knowledge and assign asterisks (*) to the areas where you still need information from your prospective employer.

Questions the Employer Should Answer

① Have you offered this position to anyone before me?

② If yes, what were the circumstances surrounding the match that led you to make an offer?

③ Can you share with me why the offer was turned down?

④ From my background and experience, what has represented the best match for what you are looking for?

⑤ What is the history of this position?

- How many people have held this position? _____
  _____

- How is this role valued compared with other roles in the organization? _____
  _____

- What did the person who held the position most recently go on to? _____
  _____

- With respect to this role, are there developments, initiatives, or changes you would like to see implemented? _____
  _____

After you have completed the *Offer Analysis*, use the following checklist to determine whether or not you should negotiate:

CHECKLIST FOR DETERMINING WHEN
AND WHEN NOT TO NEGOTIATE

Key Item	Yes ☺	No ☹	Maybe 😐	Need More Information
Enough of my *five top identified core priorities and professional values* are reflected in this offer to make negotiating the next logical step.	___	___	___	___

Why I know this: _____

_____

_____

| I know that they are 100% committed to this offer. | ___ | ___ | ___ | ___ |

Why I know this: _____

_____

_____

| I know that they are strongly invested in having me join their organization. | ___ | ___ | ___ | ___ |

Why I know this: _____

_____

_____

| They are close enough in the terms of the offer to make negotiating a worthwhile effort. | ___ | ___ | ___ | ___ |

Why I know this: _____

_____

_____

Action Items

**Check
When
Completed**

_____ Congratulate and reward yourself on the milestone of receiving a job offer!

_____ Recognize that the choice of when and when not to negotiate is ultimately yours.

_____ Before deciding whether and/or when to negotiate, engage in a thorough reexamination of your core professional values:

Refer back to self-critique in Chapter 1.

Complete the *Professional Priority Spectrum* in this chapter independent of any other offer you have in hand.

Prioritize your five most critical core values based on this exercise.

_____ Examine and summarize the points of the job offer itself, both subjective and objective factors, and complete the *Offer Analysis, Parts I and II*, in this chapter.

_____ Tie all the preceding material into the final checklist for determining when and when not to negotiate.

Know thine opportunity.

PI HACUS, 700–600 BC
THE INTERNATIONAL THESAURUS OF QUOTATIONS, 1996, P. 480,
NEW YORK: HARPERCOLLINS

CHAPTER **8**	***Outlining Potential Negotiation Scenarios: Acceptable and Unacceptable Outcomes***

Agenda

- Why preparation is essential.

- "If/Then" scenarios.

- What is "unacceptable" and why.

- Managing the process when you have a counteroffer.

- Max's Story.

Anybody can do just about anything with himself that he really wants to and makes up his mind to do. We are capable of greater things than we realize. How much one actually achieves depends largely on: (1) Desire, (2) Faith, (3) Persistent effort, (4) Ability. But if you are lacking the first three factors, your ability will not balance out the lack. So concentrate on the first three and the results will amaze you.

NORMAN VINCENT PEALE
HAVE A GREAT DAY—EVERY DAY, 1985

Date:	Today
To:	Everyone Who Is Willing to Prepare for Success
Subject:	How to Project into the Future to Get What You Need in the Present

PREPARATION

Active, concentrated, and careful *preparation* will translate into confidence and composure when you are faced with the challenge of thinking on your feet. It is harder to retrace your steps *after* you have agreed to something than it is to be well prepared *before* you even begin the discussion! Among the people who proactively plan for a negotiation, the majority report that they are successful in achieving their goals in the negotiation process and that, if they have to walk away from the opportunity because there is no room for compromise on the employer's side, they have peace of mind because they know that they have given the negotiation process their best effort. They have fewer regrets.

It might not seem natural or comfortable to take all the steps outlined in this section, but if you persevere, you will avoid the pitfalls that plague people who attempt to negotiate on their own behalf.

Pay close attention to the preparation part of this process. Analyzing and evaluating are essential steps in the flow of work needed before you negotiate, but the *preparation phase involves action before engaging in the dynamic negotiation process.*

Do not skip this section and this work: Preparation is a *must.* Your preparation will only be as useful as the quality of the work and the time that you have put into the analytical and evaluative parts of the negotiation process. This step requires that you project yourself into the future and explore several possible "if/then" scenarios. These will open up your thinking to areas of trade-offs. Some examples of "if/then" scenarios are on page 72.

If you are the kind of person who tends to rely on facts when preparing for eventualities, you will have to **stretch** beyond what you are usually comfortable with and consider the possibilities.

If . . .	Then . . .
I could start in September after my planned summer vacation . . .	I would have more flexibility on the amount of a sign-on bonus to join this employer.
I could telecommute one day a week . . .	I would be willing to trade off $XX in my base salary because it would enhance my quality of life and reduce my high commuting costs somewhat.
I can negotiate for a pay review in six months instead of a year . . .	I would accept the starting salary as offered.
I can travel 10% of the time rather than 25% . . .	I would settle for less in salary.

Fill in the remaining sections with your "if/then" scenarios.

Put yourself in a creative, flexible frame of mind, then work through the following exercise to hone your projection skills. Start by answering, to the best of your ability, these questions:

• What is unacceptable to me? _____

_____

_____

• If I were to say "thank you, but no thank you," what would that look like? What might the conditions be? _____

_____

_____

• Where is my limit for:
Job responsibilities *(what am I unwilling to assume)?* _____

_____

_____

Corporate culture? _____

_____

_____

Benefits? _____

_____

_____

Vacation? _____

_____

_____

Profit sharing? _____

_____

_____

401(k)? _____

_____

_____

Base compensation? _____

_____

_____

Percentage of travel? _____

_____

_____

Reporting relationship? _____

_____

_____

Your limit might be a highly fluid variable. It will be influenced by numerous dynamics:

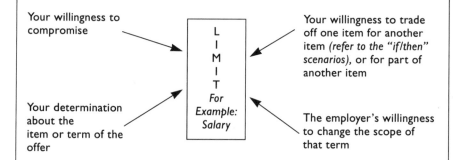

As you think about it, your limit could become a moving target depending on which influence is stronger. Be as clear and definitive about each limit as possible. The definition of each item will enable you to be flexible when you need to weigh multiple influences. Answer the following questions (Step 1):

STEP I

What would an *acceptable* offer look like and why?

1. Check your motivation
2. Check your ego needs *(Be careful!)*
3. Check your assumptions
4. Monitor your emotional motivations

What would the timing of the offer need to be and why? _____

_____

_____

What would the base compensation need to be? _____

_____

_____

What would the benefits need to be and why? _____

_____

_____

Now that you have outlined the basic information for what an acceptable offer should look like, do the same for an unacceptable offer, Step 2 on page 76.

If you do not have enough information to answer why these would be acceptable or unacceptable outcomes, pause long enough to check your motivations, assumptions, and expectations and your gut reaction or emotional response. Use the following questions to prompt you in getting the right information:

① What do you need to know to understand what the employer's position might be *(refer back to Chapter 5)?*

Step 2

What would an *unacceptable* offer look like and why?

• Responsibilities *(functional/departmental):* _____

_____

_____

• *Timing of start date:* _____

_____

_____

• *Title:* _____

_____

_____

• *Compensation:* _____

_____

_____

• *Bonus(es):* _____

_____

_____

• *Benefits:* _____

_____

_____

• *Career progression:* _____

_____

_____

② How can I safeguard the quality of the dialogue and the business relationship while standing firm on what is important to me in this situation?

③ What do I really want? Why?

④ What alternative approaches could I use *(see exercises in Chapter 16)?*

⑤ What could I accept but would be second best?

⑥ What would represent flexibility on my part and would allow me to attain what I feel strongly about?

⑦ At what point do I need to close the discussion and turn down the offer?

Watch Out: If you are too narrow in your assessment of the situation, you will lock yourself in.

HOW DO YOU HANDLE MORE THAN ONE OFFER?

Thought Starters

- Is it appropriate to leverage one offer against another?
- Might you offend the employer if you use the weight of a second offer?
- Will you jeopardize the offer if you bring in the details of the less preferred offer?

Everyone hopes to be in the driver's seat when receiving a job offer. When two offers come through, it can be an intoxicating experience. If you have ever been recruited simultaneously for two positions, you will be able to identify with the temptation to wield what might be an inflated sense of power and control. If you are not careful, you can come across as brash, arrogant, and overly confident. Remember that you always need to balance the specific terms of the offer with the relationship aspects of the offer. The following case reflects the dynamics involved in leveraging one offer against another:

Max's Story

Max, an accomplished, mid-level human resources professional, worked for a company located $3\frac{1}{2}$ hours away from where he lived. The job and the company were right for him and suited him in his professional life but he felt that the sacrifice he was making in his personal life was becoming increasingly difficult to justify. Max commuted home every weekend, but it was becoming harder to be away from his family during the week.

When Max got a telephone call from a recruiter about a local opportunity, he was intrigued. The salary was lower than he was currently earning, but the job was 20 minutes from his home and family. He felt that he had to explore the opportunity. His profile and credentials were ideal for the employer and the job. The magnetic pull of the company's proximity to his home made the situation seem ideal.

When Max went in to interview, he found the alignment between the requirements of the job and his abilities to be almost perfect. He knew that he would be able to do the job and that he would also have room to grow. He saw some initial issues regarding management and communication style but glossed over them because other factors, like the commute, were so positive.

Position Specifications	Max's Professional Capabilities
• Work as part of a senior level multifunctional team.	• Six years' experience as a functional leader for Human Resources in a large corporation.
• Establish priorities for training for entire company.	• Created training function for a workforce of 200.
• Review and establish criteria for upgraded benefits program.	• Oversaw the benefits program for 300 exempt and nonexempt employees.
• Prepare/train first-level supervisors in team-based principles and behaviors.	• Steward for all team-building programs for 300 employees.
• Establish best practices in hiring and incorporate in Standard Operating Procedures (SOPs) for all managers.	• Instituted SOPs for interviewing and hiring for 100 managers.

The second offer (often referred to as a "counteroffer") came in from his employer. He was highly valued by his employer, and they did not want to lose his expertise and skill. When he told his boss that he wanted to leave the company to take another job closer to his home, he was given an immediate raise. Tempted as he was to be swayed by the overture, he made it clear that the quality-of-life issues took precedence for him. They knew about the hardship he experienced by being away from his family during the week and commuting home every weekend, but selfishly, they also wanted him to remain in his job with them. Max felt somewhat torn because he wanted to be loyal to his employer, but he also needed to respect his personal needs and the needs of his family.

Through the recruiter, he asked for a higher salary. He received the increase and decided to accept the offer. Within 48 hours of telling his employer that he was going to accept the offer at the company near his home, they made another counteroffer. He rejected the counteroffer and went to work for the new company.

To his surprise, the realities of starting a new job with a new company were jolting. Max was not ready for the magnitude of change facing him. His former employer kept calling him to "woo" him back and, within a week when he received a third counteroffer, Max decided to leave the new company and to rejoin his former employer.

There are several lessons to be learned from Max's experience:

- *Max let himself be confused.* He knew that if he got more money from the company that wanted to recruit him, the compensation and proximity would lead him to take the job. Though he leveraged one offer against the other and was successful, he did not focus on the facts that suggested the *new company culture was not right for him.* He was caught up in the idea that he would have a better quality of life and *he dismissed the importance of the cultural fit.* On paper, it looked like a very good match but, in actuality, it was not a good fit. The management style was too formal and rigid for him and the communication style was the exact opposite of what he wanted. But, in his feeling of relief at finally reconciling his personal life with his work life, he ignored a major aspect of the picture.

- *Max tarnished his professional reputation by leaving the new company within a week* of having started the new job. He appeared immature and hasty in his decision making. He created havoc for himself and for the new company.

- When Max rejoined his former employer, not only did he have to *live up to the new expectations (which went along with the three salary increases),* but personally he had to come to terms with having left the new employer in the lurch. He had misled them and violated a fundamental principle of safeguarding his professional reputation.

Leveraging one offer against another can work to your advantage, but you have to use the process outlined in Chapter 1 *(Establishing Job/Career Selection Priorities)* and stay focused on what is important to you. Go through the self-inventory and hold onto a clear sense of what you value most highly. The realm of offers and counteroffers has a lot of pull and, without a grounding in your conviction about priorities, you can steer off course very easily. Slipping into egotistical posturing behavior happens too often in situations where one offer is leveraged against another. Stay focused on the essential priorities and be very careful if you use one offer to gain advantage over another offer.

Action Items

**Check
When
Completed**

_____ Develop your own "If/Then" scenarios.

_____ Address questions about "What is
unacceptable."

_____ Review the sensitivities required when working
with a counteroffer.

_____ Read Max's Story.

*Discovery consists of seeing what everybody has seen, and
thinking what nobody else has thought.*

ALBERT SZENT-GYORGI
THE OXFORD DICTIONARY OF MODERN QUOTATIONS, 1991,
EDITED BY TONY AUGARDE, OXFORD, ENGLAND:
OXFORD UNIVERSITY PRESS

Anticipating Points of Agreement and Disagreement

Agenda

- Maintain open communication.

- Identify roadblocks that will impede your discussion.

- How to handle discussions on a cellular phone.

- Warnings and special preparations when negotiating over the telephone.

- Conditions you *need* to create for the discussion.

- Checklist for *Conducting a Negotiation over the Telephone.*

Luck is what happens when preparation meets opportunity.

DARRELL ROYAL
AMERICAN HERITAGE DICTIONARY OF QUOTATIONS,
MARGARET MINER AND HUGH RAWSON,
1997, P. 292, NEW YORK: PENGUIN

Date: Today

To: Negotiators Who Want to Prepare for Success

Subject: How to Thoroughly Rehearse for the Final Act

In preparing for the actual discussion, you need to anticipate areas in which you and the potential employer might find agreement *(and why)* and areas in which you might find disagreement *(and why)*. Examining and preparing for these areas ahead of time will better equip you in handling some possible friction during the actual discussion.

The preparation phase has six goals:

① Identify the ways in which you can maintain open, constructive flows of information.

> **Example**: *Use good eye contact, thank them for the offer, maintain composure and calm to cultivate a good atmosphere.*

② Pinpoint the roadblocks in the flow of communication that might arise because of the employer's issues or concerns.

> **Example**: *Discomfort for the employer because of lack of authority in changing the terms of the offer. Employer would feel disempowered.*

③ Plan phrases (Chapter 10) and wording that will help neutralize the employer's issues and the resulting roadblocks.

> **Example:** *I can appreciate the pressure you must be under. I would like to find a way for us to resolve this area of concern. In what way could we incorporate flexibility around this?*

④ Pinpoint the roadblocks in the flow of communication that might arise because of *your* concerns or issues.

> **Example:** *Becoming tuned in to underlying assumptions and expectations (important).*
>
> *Knowing how to place emphasis in the right place.*

⑤ *Plan reminders* to yourself about priorities you want to attend to and alternative creative ways to work with the priorities *(see the Priorities Plan chart in this chapter).*

PRIORITIES PLAN

Your Priorities	Employer's Viewpoint		My Viewpoint	
	Concerns and Issues	My Plan	Personal Issues	My Plan
1. Six-week delay in start date. Why? Current commitments at work plus a planned 2-week vacation.	"We need someone right away. We have had this vacancy far too long already."	Tell them that I will start to learn about the job by studying all the reports and literature they can give me.	I do not want to compromise on this. It would create havoc in my plans and I would lose money.	Reassure them that I will be a strong contributor in six weeks (actually a better one) because I will be able to focus after I am refreshed. Also I am willing to adjust my start date by a few days. (There will be a psychological benefit for the employer.)
Fill in your information here. 2. Why? 3. Why? 4. Why?				

⑥ *Rehearse* your outline:

    a. For handling employer issues you anticipate arising and addressing the issues without creating friction.

    b. For handling your own emotionally charged issues, which could disrupt the flow of communication.

    Example: *A start date: You are not willing to go to work for them for six weeks. You assume they will put pressure on you to begin working for them sooner.*

Go back to Chapter 1 to review your priorities, to Chapter 3 to incorporate what you know about the terms of the offer, and to Chapter 5 to incorporate the needs and goals of the employer.

Completing the *Priorities Plan* on the following page will help you apply the lessons you have learned so far. In the first column, list the items you wish to accomplish *(in order of importance)* and why each is important to you. In the second column, anticipate the concerns and issues that the employer may voice in opposition to your goal. The third column provides a place for your plan to deal with each issue. In the fourth column, outline your own issues and problems that relate to your priority. The final column provides a place for notes on how you might adjust your priorities to deal with employer objections.

Review the example on page 84 first, then create your own list.

The *Priorities Plan* will equip you with good strategy. But what about conducting the discussion over the telephone? The following section addresses the idiosyncrasies that creep in when you are maneuvering the maze of a negotiation over the telephone.

Using the Telephone, a Computer, a Car Phone, or a Calculator When Discussing the Final Terms of an Offer— Warnings and Special Preparations

The telephone, a computer, a calculator, and a cellular phone are commonplace adjuncts in most business transactions *and* often are essential to the process. Consider just a few of the ways that today's technology can filter into a negotiation scenario, and the following questions and answers take on immediate significance:

What are the Watch Outs! when discussing sensitive, delicate matters over the telephone?
Pace yourself . . . do not rush . . . make sure that you have enough time. Establish an appointed time for talking about your offer, if possible, avoid discussing salary and bonuses over the telephone. Have paper, a pencil, a calculator, and a calendar at your disposal.

How can the information you might have kept on the computer be of best use to you when you are conducting a high-stakes negotiation?
If you have notes from previous conversations and interviews, use them here.

What do you need to do if you find yourself on a cellular phone trying to concentrate on the facts and details of a serious discussion, and you are also driving?
Pull over to the side of the road! Do not try to negotiate and drive at the same time.

When should you have a calculator with you and how can you best use it?
A calculator will be most useful when you are calculating salary and/or bonus figures.

What can you do to create the best conditions for the discussion using the technology available?
Make sure that you have no interruptions!

These are just a few of the questions to anticipate before you launch into a full and open dialogue, especially with the added obstacle of the telephone as your primary communication medium. When you conduct a negotiation over the telephone you sacrifice the opportunity to observe the other person's nonverbal reactions. Without these cues from body language, you could make erroneous assumptions. You'll need to be vigilant about preparing for the discussion. Do not underestimate how difficult the negotiation process can become. The following are key areas for consideration.

Conditions

① If you know that you will be conducting the negotiation over the phone, *create* a time and place that will be conducive to the singular focus of the discussion. *Do not plan to call from the car while driving.*

② *Eliminate* all distractions *(i.e., work only on the discussion at hand).*

③ *Use* the checklist in this chapter to ensure that you are organized and prepared for total concentration on the conversation.

④ *Prepare* two or three acceptable alternatives for the discussion. Calculate what you are willing to adjust in exercising flexibility.

⑤ *Listen* to the person on the other end of the phone carefully. Take notes while the person is talking to you. It is *very* easy to be distracted when representing yourself on the telephone. The more distracted you are, the more challenging it will be to listen to the other person.

⑥ *Be prepared* with questions.

⑦ *Anticipate* the employer's questions and prepare by having answers ready.

⑧ *Make* clear the amount of time you will use to conduct this discussion. You need to agree with the employer's representative about the length of time he or she has available and that you have available:

Employer: Hi, Ann. We would like to offer you the position.
You: Hi, thank you for calling. I was hoping to get the job offer. I want to make sure that we won't be cut short in this discussion. I have a commitment in 30 minutes. Should we schedule a time to discuss the details or should we talk about them now?
Employer: Thirty minutes should be fine. If we need more time, I could continue tomorrow morning between 8:00 and 9:00.
You: Fine. Why don't we get started.

⑨ *Develop* an outline with the main points you want to cover in a logical sequence. *The outline will help you keep things clear and organized.*

⑩ If necessary, *break* the discussion down into small, distinct, and manageable parts.

Emotions quickly escalate when you are representing yourself in a negotiation over a job offer. You will do yourself a favor if you stay as organized as possible.

Dynamics

What makes these phone discussions challenging is that it feels as though "they" have more power to define the situation because they are presumably sitting in their bastion of power and represent something you want *(the job)*. Without the input of seeing facial reactions and body language, it is easy to feel at a disadvantage.

Pace yourself through the discussion. It becomes challenging to listen as well as you will need to if you become uncomfortable. Remember to stay calm. *Do not try to rush the discussion* —you will regret it if you do.

Use the following checklist on pages 89–90 as a tool in this process. It is divided into four sections: Conditions, Paperwork, Basic Essentials, and Final Items.

Customize this checklist and record information that reflects what you need in addition to what I have listed here. For each item, check the appropriate column (*Done* or *To Be Done*) and assign a date.

The true test of good negotiators is that they put enough structure and forethought into the details and the process to feel confident in handling the surprises—of which there are usually several. The structure should not stand in your way when negotiating; it should give you enough comfort and self-confidence to proceed with more ease and savvy. Responding appropriately to the unpredictable parts of a negotiation does not happen automatically for most of us. It takes a lot of preparation and planning. Though it can be more challenging to represent yourself over the telephone, with the use of an outline and the checklist approach shown here, it is possible to do it correctly and well.

CHECKLIST FOR CONDUCTING A NEGOTIATION OVER THE TELEPHONE

	Done	Date	To Be Done	Date
① Conditions:				
Privacy.	___	___	___	___
No interruptions.	___	___	___	___
Calm atmosphere.	___	___	___	___
Specific time assigned to this discussion.	___	___	___	___
No distractions (e.g., *music, second phone line, fax machine, etc.*).	___	___	___	___

Additional Reminders: _____

_____

_____

_____

	Done	Date	To Be Done	Date
② Paperwork:				
Your resume.	___	___	___	___
Position description.	___	___	___	___
Notes from previous meetings.	___	___	___	___
Correspondence to and from the employer.	___	___	___	___
Spreadsheets with 2 or 3 alternative sets of numbers.	___	___	___	___
List of questions you need to ask.	___	___	___	___
Outline with main points to be discussed.	___	___	___	___
List of questions you think the employer will ask.	___	___	___	___
List of your issues and rationales for each.	___	___	___	___
List of the employer's (anticipated) issues/concerns.	___	___	___	___
Annual report from the company.	___	___	___	___

Additional Reminders: _____

_____

_____

_____

(continued)

CHECKLIST FOR CONDUCTING A NEGOTIATION
OVER THE TELEPHONE (CONTINUED)

	Done	Date	To Be Done	Date
③ **Basic Essentials:**				
Pencil.	——	——	——	——
Pen.	——	——	——	——
Eraser.	——	——	——	——
Paper.	——	——	——	——
Calendar.	——	——	——	——
Calculator.	——	——	——	——
Computer.	——	——	——	——
Fax—with paper in it!	——	——	——	——
Mirror—to monitor your reactions!	——	——	——	——
Clock.	——	——	——	——

Additional Reminders: _____

_____

_____

_____

④ **Final Items:**

Tape recorder *(to capture the essence of the dialogue after it is over)*. Use the tape recorder *after* your discussion, not during the exchange. Capture your thoughts on the recorder or on paper the moment you hang up the telephone. —— —— —— ——

Follow-up plan *(who will write the final letter and when)*. —— —— —— ——

Additional Reminders: _____

_____

_____

_____

Action Items

**Check
When
Completed**

_____ Understand the important conditions for creating open communication.

_____ Complete the *Negotiating Priority Plan.*

_____ Identify and plan for roadblocks in the negotiation.

_____ Review the many special parameters and *Watch Outs* for negotiation via telephone.

_____ Use the *Checklist for Conducting Negotiation over the Telephone.*

There is no force so powerful as an idea whose time has come.

EVERETT DIRKSEN
AMERICAN POLITICIAN
(NOMINATING BARRY GOLDWATER FOR THE PRESIDENCY, 1964)

Preparing Phrases and Open-Ended Questions

Agenda

- Identifying important questions for the negotiation.

- Review sample dialogue during the preliminary phase of the negotiation.

- Analyzing and incorporating into your phrases the ways in which the offer has been constructed.

- Anatomy of the position and its importance in your strategy.

- Review Question Data Bank.

- Designing questions and phrases that tap into the employer's priorities.

The difference between the almost right word and the right word is really a large matter—'tis the difference between the lightning bug and the lightning.

MARK TWAIN (SAMUEL L. CLEMENS)
THE NEW INTERNATIONAL DICTIONARY OF QUOTATIONS,
2ND EDITION, MARGARET MINOR AND HUGH RAWSON, 1994, P. 36,
NEW YORK: SIGNET-PENGUIN GROUP

Date: Today

To: Everyone Who Needs More Answers to Negotiate the Offer

Subject: How and When to Construct and Ask All the Right Questions

---

What does it take to open the lines of discussion? Generally speaking, asking thoughtful, pointed questions that generate substantive—not pat—answers is the key to setting a productive negotiation in motion.

Open-ended questions will elicit more information from the employer than closed-ended questions. It will take you more time to construct good open-ended questions, but it will result in the acquisition of more data. Your aim at this point in the process will be to invite as much disclosure as possible. Here are just a few comparisons between closed-ended and open-ended questions:

Closed:

Are you satisfied with the performance results in the department?

The other person can answer "yes" or "no."

Open:

In what way(s) have the performance results in the department been satisfactory or unsatisfactory?

This question requires that the other person give more than a superficial and/or cursory answer. It also potentially gives you, as the person wanting more insight into the way the employer thinks, a clearer understanding of the company's priorities and goals.

Closed:

You interviewed other candidates for this position; why have you offered the position to me?

You will get some valuable feedback from the response to this question, but you could get *more* information from an open-ended question format.

Open:

In what ways does my background fit with your priorities for this department/division? Which accomplishments interest you the most and why?

Answers to these questions could reveal a great deal about what the employer values most and why.

Closed:

Can you change the base compensation?

The phrasing of this important question leads to more pressure for you. You would commonly find the following sequence of questions and answers:

You: *(Request)* Can you change the base compensation?
Employer: *(Objection)* What do you have in mind?
You: Well, the base salary is 15 percent less than what I am currently making.
Employer: We have not typically increased the base compensation. If we did it this time, it would set a precedent.
You: Who would you need to work through to create the change?
Employer: Let me talk with my boss and get back to you tomorrow.

Notice how stilted this exchange seems. Also, notice how the burden to keep this a priority is on the candidate.

Closed:

I would like to reevaluate the base compensation part of the offer.

You and the employer are on opposite ends of a spectrum:

Open:
In what ways could we reevaluate the base compensation part of the offer?

You and the employer are *together* looking at ways to address the issue:

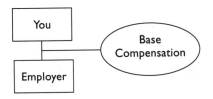

The dialogue might look like this:

You: First, I want to acknowledge the time and thought that went into *your* extending this offer. I am very enthusiastic, and there is one remaining issue that I hope we can resolve together.

Employer: Thank you for your insight and positive attitude. What issue can we work on?

You: The base salary is lower than what I am currently making, and I would like to know what was factored into the base compensation part of the offer.

Employer: This has been the standard level of compensation for this position for the past several years.

You: Are there ways in which we could include more in the base pay so that I do not have to take a 15 percent pay cut?

Employer: Well, we've never done that, but since you are our top candidate for the position, we could look into it.

You: Thank you. I know that the match is strong between what you are looking for and what I could contribute. I would like to work for you and want to do what I can to create a good situation.

Employer: This might take a couple of meetings. I'll get back to you within the next couple of days.

You: I look forward to hearing from you.

Your goal is to open up the discussion and create possibilities. You can't do this effectively if you are too rigid and firm. Prepare to ask several questions and to create a common focus of resolving an issue together.

During the last part of the interview process, ask some of the following questions to develop a clear understanding about what the employer is thinking:

Priority: To set up a way of getting a better understanding of what the employer is thinking while keeping an open and comfortable atmosphere

- Please describe the profile of success in your unit/organization.

- How long has this position been vacant?

- What is the history of this position?

- Have there been major differences in the ways that people have fulfilled the duties and responsibilities of the position?

- What has worked well?

- What would you like to see done differently?

Questions you might ask after receiving the offer:

- Given your priorities and given my interest in the position and the organization, please share with me where flexibility might exist.
- In what ways can we reshape or redefine aspects of this offer?

Take some of the following steps when preparing for the negotiation:

① Consider your typical style of communicating *(e.g., are you usually good at getting complete information or do you find that you have to go back several times to fill in the gaps and get more details).*

② Proactively figure out how you can get at the information you need *(use the questions in Chapters 6 and 19 as you plan your strategy).*

③ Figure out where the gaps in information are likely to be and plan phrases around the gaps *(e.g., you won't have access to how the employer arrives at an offer. Develop questions that will help you understand the process used to construct the offer).*

Use the following *Question Data Bank* to structure your thoughts about what you need to know. Refer to Chapters 1, 6, 15, and 19 to explore questions and resources. Pay close attention to the *Career Priority*

QUESTION DATA BANK

Check When Done	Topic	Questions	When	Who
_____	Position	How would you describe the priorities in this position?	Interview	Hiring Manager
_____	Reporting Relationship	How would you characterize the reporting relationship? Formal, informal, structured, or open door?	Interview	Hiring Manager
_____	Work Environment	How would you describe the work environment?	Interview	Hiring Manager
_____	Definition of Success	How would you describe your short-term and mid-term goals for the department?	Interview/ Negotiation	Hiring Manager/ Future Colleagues
_____	Bonus	In what ways are incentives aligned with expected results?	After an Offer Is Received	Hiring Manager/ Future Colleagues
_____	Vacation	Is the length of vacation adequate?	After an Offer Is Received	Hiring Manager/ Human Resources
_____	Base Salary	How have you approached the base salary for this position?	After an Offer Is Received	Hiring Manager/ Human Resources
_____	Benefits	Please describe your benefits package.	After an Offer Is Received	Human Resources
_____	Pension	How does your pension plan work?	After an Offer Is Received	Human Resources
_____	Other	Complete this section with your own questions.		

Self-Inventory in Chapter 1. The items marked could prompt you to develop questions in your top priority areas.

The interview and negotiation process involve continuous discovery.
Just when you think you have learned as much as you could know about
the employer, new information appears. The more you learn, the more
you feel confident in your ability to maneuver and manage the negotiation process.

The closing phase is particularly sensitive because of the pivotal turn
of discussion. This is when you can experience a sudden halt to resolution of the issues or a smooth forward sense of progress.

*Remember to stay focused on the questions and to cultivate the rela-
tionship and rapport.* There are many important aspects of an offer. The
more you identify each part of the employment offer, the greater will be
your chance of including flexibility in the process.

The following chart depicts some of the more commonly established
parts of an offer.

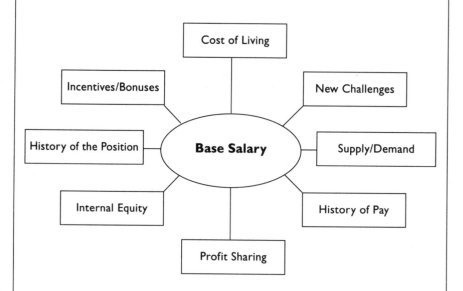

THE CLOSING: MAKING IT WORK

Use the following questions as you take the pivotal turn of trying to re-define the terms of the offer:

- In what ways can the structure of the package be changed?
- In what ways, other than compensation, can we consider changing the nature of the offer?
- Who else might need to be involved in discussions about the terms of the offer?
- In what ways can we organize the discussion so that we can reconnect after an initial discussion?

Many negotiations extend beyond one or even two meetings. Take your time as you probe for information. The clearer, more precise the questions are, the more constructive will be the dialogue.

It is extremely easy to get stuck as you probe for information. Use the *Question Data Bank* chart to avoid the escalation of uncomfortable feelings, which often result in ineffective exchanges. The stakes are high—this is your career and a sizable portion of your time and energy is about to be dedicated to a company.

With precise language and open-ended phrases, you will be able to manage this dimension of data gathering.

Action Items

**Check
When
Completed**

_____ Develop open-ended questions and determine
what you need to know.

_____ Practice asking the questions in a role play
situation with a colleague or friend.

_____ Develop awareness of your reactions as you
rehearse the questions.

_____ Use the *Question Data Bank* to access relevant
questions at every stage of the interview and
negotiation process.

*I find the great thing in this world is not so much where we
stand, as in what direction we are moving: to reach the port
of heaven, we must sail sometimes with the wind and
sometimes against it—but we must sail, and not drift, nor
lie at anchor.*

OLIVER WENDELL HOLMES, SR.
AMERICAN HERITAGE DICTIONARY OF AMERICAN QUOTATIONS,
MARGARET MINOR AND HUGH RAWSON, 1997, P. 2,
NEW YORK: PENGUIN

PART 2

DURING

Managing the Negotiation Process with Ease and Success

*Mastering Negotiation
Skills and Strategies*

Agenda

- Defining mastery in negotiation.

- Discovering your personal negotiating profile:

    Ways to master your own negotiating style.

    Ways to integrate the best of each style.

- Preparing a Check-and-Balance List.

- Mike's Story *(a senior technical supervisor does his homework and puts checks and balances to work).*

- Creating optimal conditions for a productive negotiation.

- Checklist/Action Steps.

Let every eye negotiate for itself, and trust no agent.

WILLIAM SHAKESPEARE

Date: Today

To: Everyone Who Wants to Master Negotiation Skills with Strength and Balance

Subject: How to Represent Your Interests with Both Instinct and Knowledge

---

You are entering the discussion zone. Are you equipped to handle each twist, nuance, and turn of the exchange? If not, can you shore up your skills to gain more comfort and mastery in representing your own interests?

Mastery: (mäs´-ter-y) means the possession of consummate skill. The result, in a defined situation, is that you have a sense of confidence about your ability to respond in the right way to the right challenges. You have sufficient related experience to determine what you need to respond to and how you need to respond to it. Your direct or related experience enables you to make quick decisions about the appropriate response and the style in which you need to deliver it.

Mastery in negotiation begins with self-awareness. To get a quick handle on your natural tendencies as a negotiator and as a communicator, review the four Negotiating Profiles in the table on pages 104–105 and see which type(s) might fit your style.

WHERE DO YOU FIND YOURSELF?

If you are going to buy a car, you probably need to have some qualities of the *Skeptic* and some of the *Problem Solver.* If you exercise some of both styles, you will have a healthy critical eye when dealing with the salesperson and you would exercise a good analytical approach in arriving at the price. People who identify with the other two styles—*the Wing-It Specialists and Adventurers*—could and do buy cars, but they can find that activity to be extremely frustrating, cumbersome, and difficult.

THE FOUR COMMON NEGOTIATING PROFILES

Where Are You?			
Qualities	*Habits*	*Traps*	*Recovery Tricks*
"Wing-It" Specialists			
Spontaneous. Action oriented. Live for the moment. Dive in and think about the process later. Assume things will work out well.	Avoid planning. Avoid taking precautions. Don't enjoy working the details so ignore them.	Can be unprepared. Can come across as superficial. May rely on an "adrenaline rush" that might not appear.	Can ask for two negotiating meetings. Can bring some levity to an overly serious exchange.
Motto: *"Let's see what happens!"*			

Qualities	*Habits*	*Traps*	*Recovery Tricks*
Problem Solvers			
Cautious and planful. Work every angle carefully. Like to set a course and work it. Like to find the order in a situation and refine it.	Very methodical. Can place more value on the data than on the person with whom they are dealing.	Inflexible. Impersonal. Hard to relax with. Always busy calculating something.	Work through all the details and then only take brief notes into the negotiation and concentrate on the other person.
Motto: *"Have I looked at all the angles?*			

Qualities	*Habits*	*Traps*	*Recovery Tricks*
Adventurers			
Have a spirit of discovery. Enjoy putting form around something new and uncharted. Have a strong appetite for information and new experience. Curious.	Easily bored or distracted. If can't find something extraordinary, will discount things.	Experience frustration if they can't bring in new and exciting ideas. Avoid details and small points. Can get overly frustrated by people who don't think the way they do.	Recognize/verbalize positive actions and/or offer one or two compliments if off the track with the other party.
Motto: *"Find the new path!"*			

THE FOUR COMMON NEGOTIATING PROFILES (CONTINUED)

Where Are You?

Qualities	Habits	Traps	Recovery Tricks
Skeptics			
Suspicious of others' motives. Assume they might lose something. Generally uneasy.	Lose sight of the big picture because focus is on details. Limit themselves because they fear being taken advantage of.	Can be unnecessarily pessimistic. Can get so caught up in the details that they lack flexibility.	Can ask questions to test assumptions. Can make "friendliness" a priority in the exchange.

Motto: *"They want something—I just don't know what."*

You might say that you recognize some aspects of each of the four styles in your approach to negotiating your job offer. If you have the ability to bring the appropriate attitude to bear at the right moment, then you are in great shape. The following steps show that you need some of each attitude in a negotiation:

① Start out with an **Adventurer** attitude and approach the negotiation with some curiosity. Enjoy a sense of discovery about what you are about to get into. Look for the design in the process and bring your own style to planning the discussion. You are embarking on an adventure!

② Next, become a **Problem Solver.** Decide what you have to examine and how you need to examine it. Isolate the items that need emphasis and analysis. Enjoy the calming effect that good planning can have.

③ Then, use some of the **Skeptic** approach. The other party does want something, and it is probably somewhat different from what you want or you would not be negotiating. *Some* of the concern that you might lose something can be imported into your style. Temper the exaggerated sense of suspicion with a planning and problem-solving approach.

④ Finally, after you have completed the work of the process, go into the discussion with some of the spontaneity and dynamic energy of the **Wing-It Specialist.**

    This process requires the best of you and your abilities to be planful yet flexible; open yet goal oriented; careful yet extending. If these appear contradictory, they aren't. They are different points along a continuum. The more versatile you are, the more you will be able to influence the outcomes in this process.

    An important part of mastery involves ***trusting*** yourself and your innate sense of what "feels" right. A check-and-balance system *(check what you know and balance it with skill and what you feel)* allows you to operate in a reliable way.

A CHECK-AND-BALANCE SYSTEM

		Prompters	Your Thoughts
① Check *(What You Know)*	Appraise the *situation* and the *employer.*	→ What do they need? → Why do they need it? → What kind of person am I dealing with?	_____ _____ _____ _____ _____ _____ _____ _____
② Check *(What You Know)*	Evaluate the most important items.	→ What are the significant factors and why? → What are the important conditions that I have to pay attention to?	_____ _____ _____ _____ _____ _____ _____

(continued)

A CHECK-AND-BALANCE SYSTEM (CONTINUED)

		Prompters	Your Thoughts
③ Balance *(Skill and What You Feel)*	Determine how capable you are to handle the items and conditions.	→ Which of my experiences relate to this situation?	
		→ When have I had to communicate under pressure and have done well?	
		→ When have I done well in representing my interests with someone?	
		→ How do I feel about doing this?	
④ Balance *(Skill and What You Feel)*	Identify the frame of mind you need to be in to get a strong base of confidence.	→ What has worked well in the process up until now?	
		→ What have been the highlights in my discussions with the person I am going to negotiate with?	
		→ What are the main reasons (five or more) why the employer wants to hire me?	

Mike, a talented and experienced technical supervisor, used the *check-and-balance* system to strategize his approach to negotiating a higher base salary. His story illustrates this process in action.

MIKE'S STORY

Mike, a senior technical supervisor for a large manufacturing facility, was trying to prepare for the last phase of an interview process and a possible need to negotiate. The company he worked for had decided to sell the facility and transfer the production lines to other manufacturing sites. Mike had been with the building since it had opened and knew every bit of the 600,000-square-foot facility. He, more than anyone else, knew how to handle all the complex aspects of running the physical plant. The new owners knew that they would need someone with his expertise. They had become very familiar with him over the course of a year and finally issued him a job offer. Mike was pleased with the offer, but when asked how much he expected to make in salary, he said that he would need to work through the numbers and call them back.

In preparation for the next discussion, Mike made great efforts to come up with figures that would be appropriate. He used the following checks and balances:

Checks

- Calculated what his minimum salary would need to be by putting a budget together.
- Called companies similar to the one that had made the offer to research comparable salary ranges for the same job.
- Calculated what it would cost the employer to get someone with the specialized skills he had.

Balances

- Developed ways to begin the discussion about what he was looking for.
- Identified trade-offs that would allow him to be flexible (e.g., he did not need medical benefits and could give that up).
- Identified a trade-off the employer could make if the company could not pay what he wanted.
- Put an outline together for the discussion.

After he finished his budget and weighed the aspects of the offer he would like versus what he would not like, he called the employer back.

The person who was his contact had the authority to define and, if necessary, change the offer. Mike called her and started by expressing his interest in the organization and his appreciation for the way that he had been treated. He then shared with them what he had done to arrive at a salary range. He was clear about his strong interest in the opportunity to use all his skills and expertise in a facility he knew well.

He offered his salary range, indicating that it was negotiable. After a brief hesitation, the employer said that because Mike did not need health benefits, the dollar value for the health coverage that would have gone into his offer was going to be put into his salary. Mike and the employer settled on a salary and both parties were satisfied with the number. They then arrived at a plan for a start date and the negotiation was done.

Mike combined the preparedness of the Problem Solver with some of the flexible spirit of the Adventurer. This example shows how homework is very important in the initial phase of this process. The concrete, substantiated information and numbers are the basis for developing confidence in yourself as you go forward. It is also good in that the relationship with the employer was not harmed as Mike went into the potentially charged part of the discussion. He was able to support his numbers without insulting the employer because he had done enough research to maintain a good businesslike atmosphere.

Mike was good at incorporating flexibility around salary and benefits and that enabled him to get closer to the higher end of the salary range.

How can *you* create optimal conditions for your own negotiation outcome? Start by setting your sights and expectations according to what you know about the employer and what you know about yourself. Then, prepare yourself using the following survey. The questions have been listed in priority order.

OPTIMAL NEGOTIATING CONDITIONS SURVEY

① What are your emotional reactions to this discussion? _____

_____

_____

_____

② In what ways can you represent your interests and concerns with *conviction?* When have you been able to do this in the past? Describe: _____

_____

_____

③ How can you represent yourself, your interests, and your concerns with ***composure?*** When have you been able to do this in the past? Describe: _____

_____

_____

_____

④ Define for yourself the frame of mind you need to be in during the negotiation. How can you accomplish this? _____

_____

_____

_____

⑤ Prepare to set the stage for a ***calm, businesslike*** exchange. Describe the ideal setting: _____

_____

_____

_____

⑥ Focus on ways to enhance the business relationship while representing your needs with strength of conviction. (***Hints.*** Be clear about the points you want to make. Be gentle with the individuals with whom you are interacting.) _____

_____

_____

_____

⑦ Identify and create the conditions needed for arriving at an optimal arrangement. Concentrate on:

- Location of the meeting.

- Length of time for the discussion.

- Figure out what their expectations are and plan approaches in response to them.

- Be clear about your expectations and plan for barriers.
- Identify who should participate in the negotiation and why.
⑧ Determine who has the authority to change or redefine the terms of the offer. _____

_____

_____

_____

Each skill you possess will be important in the course of the discussion. Make sure that you are well rested when you enter the negotiation because you will have to listen intently for the meaning behind every statement that the employer makes.

Mastery of the negotiation process comes from the convergence of all the efforts outlined in the chapter.

Describe your negotiation style. What are the strengths of your style? _____

_____

_____

_____

_____

_____

What are the traps or weaknesses of your style? _____

_____

_____

_____

_____

In what situation(s) have you negotiated successfully? _____

_____

_____

_____

_____

_____

Action Items

**Check
When
Completed**

_____ Review *The Four Common Negotiating Profiles* and find the type that is most like your style as a communicator. Pay special attention to the most likely *traps* and suggested *recovery tricks* to overcome them.

_____ Study the stages at which *each* negotiating profile can help the process along, and jot down notes about where the positive attributes of each profile could potentially help in negotiating your own job offer.

_____ Complete the *Check and Balance System* exercise, using Mike's Story as a guideline.

_____ Fill out the *Optimal Negotiating Conditions Survey* to manage your own expectations and project the employer's expectations, using *both* your knowledge and instincts.

_____ Be patient with yourself! Mastery does not come overnight, but the efforts you invest in this process will make a difference—and negotiating will get easier every time.

We must combine the toughness of the serpent and the softness of the dove, a tough mind and a tender heart.

MARTIN LUTHER KING, JR.
STRENGTH TO LOVE, 1963

Working and Negotiating through an Executive Search Firm*

Agenda

- Testing your knowledge about the search profession *(a quiz)*.

- *Checklist for Evaluating Recruiters.*

- When and why employers use professional search firms.

- The most desirable candidates.

- The role search firms play in the hiring process *(the confidante and the intelligence officer)*.

- How the hiring process unfolds.

- Five ways to retain ownership of the process.

- Suggested readings.

If all pulled in one direction, the world would keel over.

YIDDISH PROVERB

---

* Contributed by Janet Reswick Long,
President, Integrity Search, Inc.

Date: Today

To: Mary Simon's Rapidly Advancing Negotiators

Subject: How to Work and Negotiate through an Executive Search Firm

---

Contributing Author's Note. When Mary Simon suggested writing a separate chapter on the role that search firms play in the dynamics of job offer negotiations, we started brainstorming about some common myths in the job marketplace. Many cups of coffee and scribbled napkin notes later, we concluded that talking about the offer stage without the broader context of what search firms do and why employers use them, might be like driving in a foreign country without directions or a road map.

Working with a search firm may seem to be complex, but this chapter is intended to strip away some of the mystique and misconceptions about the recruitment industry. Inserting a third party into what is already a challenging and often emotionally charged process can create needless stress if there is not a clear understanding of who does what. A good professional recruiter can facilitate an open flow of communication that serves both you and your prospective employer.

This chapter is not intended to speak for or cover every aspect of the recruitment industry—every firm and each recruiter brings unique perspectives and talents to the table. My hope is that you will come away with a better understanding of yet another dimension of the negotiating process and will use it to complement the insights and exercises contained in Mary Simon's wonderfully thorough—and thought-provoking—book.

THE BIG LIE

Probably the most common misconception about the recruitment industry is that search firms own and control the professional employment marketplace. You may be surprised to learn that according to Kennedy Publications, publisher of *Executive Recruiter News* and the industry's most comprehensive directory of professional search firms, in any given year, less than 15 percent of all executive and managerial positions are filled by executive recruiters.

That leaves a whopping 85 percent of professional positions to be filled through other means such as networking, personal referrals, and classified advertising—the last one probably accounting for little more than 5 percent of the total employment market.

So search firms do not own the job market . . . but you still need to understand what role they do play when they are involved—in short, what a good search firm can and can't do for you. To check your knowledge in this area, take the following True/False quiz. Check one column for each question:

	True	False

① A professional recruiter's job is to help people find new positions.

② If you are thinking about changing careers, an executive search firm is your best resource.

③ Your first conversation with a recruiter sets the tone for the rest of the relationship.

④ Only large companies use search firms to fill positions.

⑤ There are several steps you can take to establish a search firm's professional style, reputation, and integrity.

⑥ Once a recruiter steps into the picture, you can step back and rest assured that a professional is managing the process.

Answers

① *False.* Executive recruiters are paid by companies to find people who meet specific needs within their organizations.

② *False.* Companies usually engage search firms to find proven commodities; that is, people who have performed the job they need done in another setting and are looking for a linear career progression. If you are contemplating a complete career shift—and most people will at least twice in their careers—a professional career counselor can provide objective advice and diagnostic testing. A search firm with a specialty in your new career of choice may be a good resource for learning what kinds of opportunities are out there, but the recruiter will probably not personally place you in your next position.

③ *True.* A good recruiter can be an ally for the rest of your career. Even if you are not looking to change jobs right this minute, respond to a recruiter's phone call with professionalism and courtesy and offer to help as a source when you can. You will find an appreciative resource of market information on your side when you want to make a change or are simply looking for data on the employment marketplace.

④ *False.* Companies that use recruiters come in many shapes and sizes; see the section "What Kind of Companies Use Search Firms?" later in this chapter.

⑤ *True.* You are not at the mercy of unprofessional recruiters. For some ideas on doing your homework in this area, refer to the *Checklist for Evaluating Recruiters* on page 118.

At the same time, be aware that:

- The recruiter may not be permitted to share the name of his or her client on an initial contact.
- If the opportunity presented is not of direct interest to you, you can lay the groundwork for a continuing relationship with this recruiter by offering to provide basic data about yourself and by suggesting other individuals who might be qualified for the opportunity at hand.

⑥ *False!* Remember that you are still in charge of your own destiny. A good recruiter can present you with a viable opportunity and facilitate a comprehensive communication process with a prospective employer. But you cannot abdicate control for your own career choices or expect the recruiter to take over your "think work," as discussed in the rest of this book.

CHECKLIST FOR EVALUATING RECRUITERS

_____ Ask the recruiter to clearly identify which firm he or she is affiliated with; request address, telephone, and fax information that you can verify. Don't hesitate to ask the recruiter to send you his or her card and some background about the search firm.

_____ Check industry source books such as Kennedy's *Directory of Executive Recruiters* to see how the search firm characterizes itself and its areas of specialty.

_____ If you are targeting a specific geographic area, check out the local chamber of commerce membership directory for search firms that are members.

_____ Ascertain what professional associations the recruiter belongs to, whether they are tied to the recruitment industry and whether the recruiter has areas of specialization.

_____ Verify that the client the recruiter claims to be representing pays the search fee—not you, the candidate. *Note. This will not be an issue for a professional search firm; the "Watch Out" is for employment agencies or career services centers that may charge the candidate.*

_____ Ask the recruiter to explain the process for conducting this search. Pay particular attention to areas such as thorough knowledge of the client and the opportunity, sensitivity to your time and privacy constraints, and overall professionalism versus high-pressure tactics.

If you agree to be presented for this particular opportunity, verify that the recruiter will:

_____ a. Protect your confidentiality.

_____ b. Not submit your credentials for any other opportunities that may arise without first obtaining your permission.

WHEN AND WHY EMPLOYERS USE
PROFESSIONAL SEARCH FIRMS

Employers have many reasons for bringing in a professional search firm to help them fill an open position. Because an employer will typically pay between 20 and 35 percent of a candidate's first-year compensation in search firm fees, there needs to be ample justification to ask for this assistance.

The most typical reasons companies engage a search firm are the following:

- *Lack of time/resources.* The company may not have the in-house capability to conduct a thorough, proactive search for qualified candidates.

- *More freedom to recruit through an independent third party.* It may be awkward, or in some cases, not permitted, for a company to directly recruit from another. A recruiter can act as a buffer and maintain discretion throughout the process.

- *"It is easier to buy it than to build it."* Search firms typically have not only the staff resources but also a strong existing network of sources and candidates in a given industry, staff function, or geographic area.

- *Qualified candidates may not be actively looking.* A recruiter can cultivate and persuade these potential candidates through proactive, personal contact. *(One of my mentors in this business, W. Lyles Carr III, likens this process to calling prospects and actually **reading** them the want ad!)*

- *Company confidentiality.* Companies may not want their competitors, their investors, or even their own employees to know that they are creating a new division or position, or replacing an individual, until the new hire is finalized.

- *Supply/demand of candidate pool.* Especially in booming industry areas, a company may initiate an all-out search to leverage as many resources as possible. One of the great paradoxes of the current economy is that the simultaneous trend toward downsizing parallels an almost unprecedented hiring boom in areas such as high technology, management consulting, and financial services.

- *Complexity of the search.* Will the position require a major relocation to an area that may be considered a trade-off for various reasons? Does the ideal candidate need to have a rare skill set involving language fluency or computer expertise? Does the company have well-publicized corporate image problems that may make the opportunity a tougher sell to qualified candidates?

All these issues and many more impact a company's decision to bring in a professional search firm.

WHICH COMPANIES USE SEARCH FIRMS?

The simplest answer might be any company that has enough motivation to hire and that is confronting any combination of the previously mentioned hiring challenges. Companies that use search firms are likely to fall into one of the following categories:

Fortune 500 Hire Top Talent

- Large corporations for whom hiring and replacing individuals is an ongoing cost of doing business. Executive search firms can help attract the caliber of candidates that will keep them even with—and ideally ahead of—their competitors.

Consulting: The New Hot Career

- Midsize and larger firms that provide services to these corporations. For example, in the information technology industry, Big six management consulting firms such as Andersen Consulting, Ernst & Young, and Coopers & Lybrand are literally hiring thousands of individuals every year to manage the installation of core operating systems.

INC's Fastest-Growing Companies on Hiring Spree

- Small, fast-growing companies in highly competitive industries. According to R. Linda Resnick, president of CEO Resources, Inc., a retained search and consulting firm, companies with 500 employees or less that are technology-based or venture-backed are the most likely candidates for retaining the services of a search firm. "The high-tech companies do—they have to," says Resnick.

WHO ARE THE TYPICAL OR IDEAL
CANDIDATES FROM A SEARCH FIRM'S STANDPOINT?

Again, the simplest answer is those candidates who are working in geographic areas, functions, or industries where the marketplace dictates the highest demand at any given time. And although conventional wisdom may be that recruiters are only interested in high-profile individuals who are earning well into the six figures, nothing could be farther from the truth. In fact, the competition for talented mid-level professionals in high-growth industries can be fierce.

My own company frequently recruits mid-management-level marketing and communications professionals in the mutual funds industry. This field is so hot that many individuals we talk to are receiving five or more calls from search firms about similar opportunities per week! And recruiters working with information technology companies report that this level of competition for qualified candidates extends to the entry level. Another reason that search firms covet talented mid-level professionals is that they are less visible than senior executives and therefore more challenging to identify.

Whatever industry specialty, compensation level, or geographic lines divide search firms, most are unified in their perceptions of what constitutes a desirable candidate. Some of the characteristics may surprise you. Following is a representative list:

Can Do! Has the candidate already proven that he or she can successfully carry out the responsibilities that are critical to this position? Nothing speaks like results in comparable fields or circumstances. Clients pay search firms to find proven commodities because it lowers the risk of hiring. This is why candidates from a direct competitor typically top a client's wish list.

Wants to Do! Does the candidate have a logical reason to accept this position? Does it make sense as a next career step? Clients tend to be skeptical of candidates who are interested only in moving for more money because they could easily be recruited again and therefore may be shorter-term hires.

What's Missing? Is there something missing (again, besides more money) in the candidate's current or most recent situation that would be satisfied by this opportunity? Even when approaching and courting you as a candidate, the recruiter wants to be assured that there is a sincere motivation on your part, that this is not merely a shopping expedition or a way to force a counteroffer from your current employer.

Good Fit? Beyond core qualifications and sincerity, is there a perceived match or fit with the client's "culture"? For example, does the client place a high value on team participation while the qualified candidate is really more of a Lone Ranger? Does the qualified candidate prefer to work in a more defined and structured environment while the client is looking for someone who thrives on open management and constant change?

Good Communication with Recruiter? Does the candidate demonstrate such qualities as courtesy, responsiveness, and good communication in interactions with the search firm? A candidate who behaves curtly or inappropriately with a recruiter during the hiring process raises a red flag and quickly loses credibility. Beyond the recruiter's own reaction to such a candidate, he or she may infer that any negative behaviors could translate to the client's work environment.

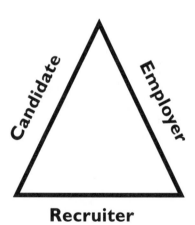

WHAT ROLE DO SEARCH FIRMS REALLY PLAY IN THE HIRING PROCESS? (WHO IS IN CHARGE HERE ANYWAY?)

In a word—**You!** *This is still your process!* A recruiter can be an excellent intermediary, but you are still responsible for assessing your own core criteria against the opportunity at hand *(see Chapter 4)*. No recruiter can—or should—attempt to make career decisions for you. You hold the reins, but to effectively harness the energy of the recruiter, you need to understand this new communication *triad (you, the prospective employer, and the recruiter)*. The flow of communication will incorporate some additional steps in the hiring process.

To get a quick picture of how the recruiter interacts with both principals—you and the prospective employer—Lyles Carr offers that on the candidate's side, the recruiter may serve as an adviser and confidante; on the employer's side, as an intelligence officer. As he so colorfully puts it, "Even George Patton, brash as he was, would not have launched his troops without good G-2" (code for intelligence).

DUAL ROLES OF THE RECRUITER

Confidante	Intelligence Officer
As a Confidante to Candidate, a Good Recruiter Can . . .	*As an Intelligence Officer to Company, a Good Recruiter Can . . .*
• Advise the candidate throughout the process with both objectivity and compassion. Is this a career move that makes sense for you? Have you considered the personal impact of this move? What other bases do you need to cover?	• Comb the marketplace for covered industry knowledge and connections to hard-to-find candidates.
• Help you think through your position as an excellent sounding board.	• Help the employer discern which candidates are both qualified for the opportunity and sincere in their interest.
• Float trial balloons to the employer in the negotiation process and provide feedback.	• Serve as a knowledgeable sounding board to examine all angles as critical choices need to be made throughout the process.

Remember that although the employer pays the search firm, a good recruiter also advocates for the candidate's needs and interests. Forcing a bad fit to make the deal won't serve either you or your prospective employer, and the recruiter's relationship with that client and overall reputation in the industry depends on a consistent track record, not a single placement.

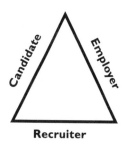
Recruiter

In the candidate/employer/recruiter triad, the recruiter is a link in the hiring chain that becomes less prominent as the candidate and the new employer gradually solidify their relationship. By the time the hire is consummated, the candidate/employer links connect, while the recruiter—initially the only bridge between the two—recedes to a follow-up and advisory role to make sure that both parties are thriving in the new relationship. *This is often a fine balancing act for the recruiter whose goal is not to make decisions for either party but to facilitate open communication in such a way that difficult decisions can be made.*

When a Recruiter Calls . . . How the Hiring Process Unfolds

The company has a need—brings in a recruiter. The recruiter reviews the position description, focuses on key marketing points to prospective candidates, and discusses target candidates, both generically and specifically (see the chart on pp. 125–126).

Important: *Enhanced communication is the key advantage of negotiating through a third party.* If you use the recruiter to your advantage, rather than being hit by "an offer from the black hole" at the end of the process, you can prepare and negotiate all along the way. If the process is working at its best, the actual offer will be almost anticlimactic! The offer will simply confirm what both parties already know and have agreed to in concept. Some employers will send a letter confirming terms of acceptance based on an oral agreement, first with the candidate through the recruiter, and then through direct conversation with the candidate.

The Hiring Process	
Process without Recruiter	*Process with Recruiter*
① Company has a need—advertises position directly to prospective candidates, cultivates colleagues, family, and others for referrals.	① Company has a need—engages search firm to identify candidates and manage hiring process. Search firm works with company's hiring manager and human resource representatives.
② Internal HR person and hiring manager screen resumes from applicants who respond to advertisements, as well as networking referrals. Selected candidates are called to set up interviews.	② Search firm proactively sources the marketplace to elicit repeated referrals to qualified candidates.
③ Company conducts first-round interviews with candidates.	③ Search firm interviews and qualifies candidates, checks initial references, and presents "short list" of candidates to client company.
④ Company brings back those candidates ranked highest by hiring manager for second (and perhaps subsequent) interviews.	④ Company selects candidates it wants to interview. Search firm informs candidates (nos as well as yesses), and facilitates necessary travel arrangements. Recruiter preps both company and candidates on interview itinerary, probes both sides for potential barriers to consummating a hire (e.g., Is candidate likely to take a counteroffer?)
⑤ Company checks references, extends offer directly to top-ranked candidate.	⑤ Company conducts first-round interviews.
⑥ Candidate accepts or declines. If candidate declines, company may offer position to a "runner-up" candidate, assuming there is one, or begin the process again. **Note.** It is often at this point, after internal resources and processes have been exhausted, that a search firm is brought in.	⑥ Both company and candidates funnel interview feedback through search firm. Recruiter continues to probe for interest and potential hurdles on both sides. Company informs recruiter which candidates it would like to continue in process; recruiter conveys decision to candidates—who must also decide if *they* wish to continue in process.

(continued)

The Hiring Process (continued)

Process without Recruiter	Process with Recruiter
Important Note. Some companies have highly qualified internal recruiters who may perform many of the steps typically taken by an outside search firm.	⑦ Process proceeds to second-round and, sometimes, subsequent interviews, with recruiter prepping both candidate and employer, and serving as conduit for feedback on both sides.
	⑧ Recruiter and/or company check final references. Company informs recruiter of first-choice candidate; gives recruiter green light to discuss broad parameters of offer with candidate to get initial read.
	⑨ Recruiter conveys terms of offer to candidate (usually by phone) and probes for areas of satisfaction and dissatisfaction, relaying feedback to employer.
	⑩ Offer is formally extended through recruiter, who may pave the way for direct dialogue between candidate and employer.
	⑪ Candidate accepts or declines offer. If candidate declines, offer may be extended to next-ranked finalist.
	⑫ After search is successfully closed, recruiter follows up regularly with both hiring manager and new employee to make sure expectations on both sides are being met. Depending on the structure of the search firm, the placement is "guaranteed" (i.e., firm will conduct a replacement search at no additional charge) for periods ranging from 90 days to 2 years.

THIS IS STILL YOUR PROCESS:
FIVE WAYS TO RETAIN OWNERSHIP WHEN A
THIRD PARTY IS INVOLVED IN THE NEGOTIATION

① *Resist the temptation to delegate the thought process to the recruiter.* A good recruiter can present you with a viable opportunity and facilitate all the pieces you need to make a decision, but he or she cannot decide for you. Work diligently through all the exercises in the rest of this book to stay clear on your core professional values and criteria and to measure the opportunity in front of you against them.

② *Ask the recruiter what you can expect.* Have the recruiter explain the hiring process (e.g., how many interviews/interviewers, whom you will meet with, how long it will take to get feedback between stages, whether any special tests are necessary). A good recruiter will know the process—not the outcome, *there are no crystal balls here!*—and should help put you at ease so there are no big surprises or glitches in the hiring process.

③ *Use the recruiter as a total employment resource.* Although the recruiter may not have the answers for all your concerns (e.g., question about a new geographic area), he or she should serve as a conduit to put you in touch with others who can advise you. This is part of the recruiter's job, not a favor to you.

④ *Document your conversations with the recruiter.* Take good notes during prep sessions and write down important questions as they occur to you. Find out the best times to communicate with the recruiter so that you can get the answers you need as questions arise.

⑤ *Ask the recruiter for feedback and advice throughout the process.* It's not too trivial a question to ask whether Friday is casual day and how *you* should dress. And it is not inappropriate to ask a recruiter how you might have handled one stage of an interview differently and how you can recoup, if necessary.

This is probably one of the few times in your life where you will have a third-party resource at your disposal who can allay your concerns, test the waters on your negotiating ideas and, ideally, inject some fun and camaraderie into what is usually a lengthy process.

Janet Reswick Long is the founder and president of Integrity Search, Inc., a national executive search and consulting firm based outside Philadelphia, Pennsylvania. The firm specializes in communications, human resources, and marketing recruitment for corporations and management consulting firms. She also coaches senior hiring managers and human resources executives on strategies to change the hiring process, and teaches interview skills to candidates through such venues as the University of Pennsylvania's College of General Studies program. Ms. Long was previously a principal with a large executive search firm based in Washington, DC, where she started up a full-service communications specialty practice.

Prior to entering the executive search field, Ms. Long spent 12 years in marketing communications positions in both corporate and agency settings. Most recently, she was a global marketing director for The Franklin Mint. She is a member of the International Association of Business Communicators, Public Relations Society of America, and American Society for Training and Development. Ms. Long holds a degree in English Literature from Adelphi University in Garden City, New York.

SUGGESTED READINGS

The Directory of Executive Recruiters ("Red Book"). Fitzwilliam, NH: Kennedy Publications, updated annually.

Kennedy's Pocket Guide to Working with Executive Recruiters, 1994, Fitzwilliam, NH: Kennedy Publications (for order information, call 800-531-0007).

A Big Splash in a Small Pond: Finding a Great Job in a Small Company, 1994, R. Linda Resnick. New York: Simon & Schuster (for order information, call 800-JOB-8955).

Rites of Passage at $100,000+ . . . The Insider's Guide to Executive Job Changing and Faster Career Progress, 1993, John Lucht. Viceroy Press/Henry Holt and Company.

The Career Makers, 1993, John Sibbald. New York: HarperCollins.

Get the Right Job in 60 Days or Less, 1991, Richard H. Beatty. New York: John Wiley & Sons.

The New Complete Job Search, 1992, Richard H. Beatty. New York: John Wiley & Sons.

Executive Career Guide for MBA's, 1995, Richard H. Beatty. New York: John Wiley & Sons.

Action Items

**Check
When
Completed**

_____ Complete the True/False quiz to check out your knowledge and assumptions about recruiters.

_____ Follow the suggested guidelines to research a firm for your comfort level.

_____ Take through notes during conversations with the search firm throughout the hiring process.

_____ Appreciate the dual role the recruiter plays as both confidante to the candidate and intelligence officer to the employer.

_____ Review the steps of the hiring process and the flow of communication when a recruiter is involved.

Remember that you are still in charge.

Good Luck!

Trade-offs and compromises are an inevitable part of living. True, all of us should be steadfast and uncompromising about something, but only the fanatic is steadfast and uncompromising about everything.

STEPHEN L. CARTER
INTEGRITY, P. 45, NEW YORK: BASICBOOKS,
A DIVISION OF HARPERCOLLINS PUBLISHERS, 1996

Negotiating: Focus on the Quality of Communication and Rapport

Agenda

- What you have accomplished if you have received an offer.

- Handling a confrontation the right way.

- Dialogue—Redirecting focus away from the conflict and toward the areas of common interest.

- How to turn a red-alert confrontational moment into a yellow-, then green-light moment.

- Confrontation spectrum.

Am I not destroying my enemies when I make friends of them?

ABRAHAM LINCOLN

Date: Today

To: Good Communicators Who Want to Get Even Better

Subject: How to Maintain Good Quality Communication and Rapport

---

At this point, you have established yourself as a strong candidate. You have successfully answered the questions and weathered the meetings that made up the interviews. The people doing the hiring liked you, thought that you were qualified for the job, and thought that you would fit into the organization. Pat yourself on the back and take a deep breath.

With an offer before you and the prospect of a negotiated exchange looming, you are about to enter new territory with its own set of unique and unusual challenges.

If you have received an offer, here is what you have already accomplished:

- You have sold your skills and experience in a convincing way.
- You have demonstrated to the employer that you will be able to contribute to the organization.
- You have made your interviewers feel some degree of comfort with you and your personality.
- You have made them feel comfortable with you as a colleague and a contributor.
- You have convinced them that you are skilled and motivated to help them address and resolve their issues.
- You have made them feel comfortable that you would be a good representative for their organization.

Applaud your performance— it is especially noteworthy because for the majority of the population, interviewing successfully is a major challenge.

Now you have to carry the momentum that began during the interview into your negotiation exchange. The dynamics that were established during the first phases of your interviewing are your ticket to success now. Implicit in the idea of negotiation is that you will encounter some differences of opinion. Those disagreements can either be negative experiences or opportunities to redefine something and come to a new understanding and accord.

A difference of opinion is usually experienced as a negative confrontation that makes either one or both parties feel defensive. But a confrontation can be positive if handled in the right way:

- It takes strength of purpose to state your opinion or belief when faced with an opposing force. Be calm and gentle with the person and clear and focused with the issues. If you handle yourself well, you will be respected for holding to what you believe.

- When confrontation occurs, you learn more than when every idea or issue discussed is readily agreed on. Learning how you respond in the heated moment and how you can adjust your reactions once you catch yourself is extremely important. This knowledge can serve you well in all parts of your life.

- You learn how the other person reacts and that can help you resolve differences with that person in the future.

- You can learn the right way to work through conflict and confrontation. The "right" way is to concentrate your attention and the attention of the other person on a common interest. *Focusing on a common interest will shift the focus of the exchange from a point of disagreement to problem solving for a constructive area of common interest.*

For example, if you are asked by the employer to travel to client sites 30 percent of the time, what can you do? In conversation, start by identifying the important issue. In this case, travel is not the issue. The client relationship is the important issue. In the mind of the employer, travel is the main and maybe the only way to achieve the goal of personalizing or strengthening the client relationship.

Your job is to bring the focus to the relationship. You can do this by mirroring or reflecting back to the employer what you agree with in their determination about the relationship. A dialogue might look like this:

You: Megan, I can appreciate your point about the importance of paying attention to the client. Without them, we would not be in business. I have had substantial experience with great clients who in essence became friends and with difficult clients who were always problematic.

Employer: Yes. We have our share of the problem relationships. They seem to creep up in every business. How did you deal with the problem people?

You: Well, I worked hard at keeping them informed of any information that would be helpful to them. I had video teleconferences with them every month. I would send them a proposed agenda along with any pertinent information ahead of time and would ask for their feedback on the agenda. If I didn't hear back from them before our scheduled meeting, I would call them to get verbal commitment to the final agenda.

Employer: Did that work?

You: Yes. The time I spent formalizing an agenda and organizing the important issues to be discussed was time well spent. They knew that I was serious about responding to their questions and needs and I felt that we had a forum for communicating; we had a paper trail, and we agreed to keep a copy of each videotaped teleconference on file in our library. I was able to get the all-important visual cues from facial expressions and body language.

Employer: Wasn't this an expensive way to do business?

You: Interestingly enough, we costed out the video teleconferencing over a 12-month time period and compared the total cost with airfare, hotel accommodations, car rental, and lost time because of airline delays and travel time; and actually, we saved money by making fewer trips and using the available technology as an alternative.

Employer: Were there complaints from customers? How did they respond?

You: At first, they were skeptical but after meeting with them in this way a couple of times, they became more comfortable with this way of doing things.

Employer: Did you eliminate travel to client locations?

You: No. I made a visit once every six months and because we were in frequent contact, our in-person meetings were more productive and more relaxed. They felt they knew me better than they otherwise would have and I felt that I understood and knew them better.

Employer: *Well, we have always had our professionals on the road at least 30 percent of the time, but if we can take care of business effectively, take care of our clients and save money, I am willing to look at this alternative for six months.*

Notice that once the focus shifted from the issue of travel to the real issue of the client relationship, the sense of adversarial tension decreased and the sense of creative problem solving increased. The employer became curious about how issues involved in maintaining good client relationships were handled.

Use cues about the employer's style and preferences to figure out how to communicate. According to Sandler Systems, Inc., 1993, a sales management and training organization, it is estimated that 55 percent of communication is visual and body language, 38 percent is tone/diction, and

Mirroring Styles	
Their Style	**Your Complementary Response/Strategy**
Fast and impatient *(rapid speech, seemingly distracted by other things going on, presenting a brief overview about the offer rather than going over every detail, etc.).*	Efficiently get to the point: Be brief and *organized:* Top priority, and why it is important. Second priority, and why it is important. Third priority, and why it is important. Maintain focused, steady, calming eye contact. Offer a genuine compliment.
Cautious and measured *(slower rate of speech, total focus on interaction, highlighting and expanding on several details of the offer, etc.).*	Offer good detail. Take your time. Offer substantiation. Be thorough.
Warm and open *(uses friendly facial expressions, tends to use anecdotes more than plain facts when relaying information).*	Mirror this behavior: Smile genuinely. Use an upbeat, warm tone of voice.

7 percent is verbal. In the example provided, the employer was cautious and measured but also a little warm and open. You can mirror the three styles listed in the table on page 134. Mirroring, that is, imitating or responding in kind, can put the other person at ease.

HANDLING CONFRONTATION

The following confrontation zones and the accompanying confrontation spectrum provide more information about how to anticipate where issues might fall and how you might best respond to them. Think about being confronted in the following ways:

- *An escalated red zone "STOP" experience.* If you discuss one of your top priorities and you are told that nothing can be done to adjust the package (e.g., you want to discuss adjusting the salary and the employer can't budge on the numbers), you might feel halted and stymied. If you have emphasized this aspect of the offer, it will feel charged and you will likely feel threatened and defensive. You will need to **"STOP"** the direction of the discussion and go onto another topic after you have calmed down. You will need to employ the greatest strength of focus and clarity not to be pulled in by the challenge of this potentially volatile experience.

- *A heightened yellow zone "CAUTION" experience.* You find that the employer feels uncomfortable with the process of negotiating; you have brought up items that they can't influence or change, and you experience some resistance on their part. Don't be surprised if you need to continue the meeting at another time or take a break. Maintain sensitivity throughout the discussion, but particularly here.

- *A low-conflict, low-confrontation "Proceed" green zone experience.* You can flow from one point to another and experience little resistance or tension from the employer.

Before you enter the discussion, calibrate the items you will want to reconcile and label each one red, yellow, or green for the process. The following chart is an example.

CONFRONTATION SPECTRUM SAMPLE

Item	"STOP" (Red)	"CAUTION" (Yellow)	"Proceed" (Green)
Delayed start date.		✓	

Tactics when discussing:
Find a "happy medium" date in between what they want and what you want. Your willingness to adjust your date will let them know that you are trying to be flexible.

Item	"STOP" (Red)	"CAUTION" (Yellow)	"Proceed" (Green)
3 weeks vacation versus the standard 2 weeks.	✓		

Tactics when discussing:
This item will require a trade-off. If you want 3 weeks vacation and it does not create an internal equity problem, you might give up a small percentage in salary.

Item	"STOP" (Red)	"CAUTION" (Yellow)	"Proceed" (Green)
Exchange of dollar amount of medical coverage for increased base salary.	✓		

Tactics when discussing:
Benefits range anywhere from 20 to 32 percent of salary. Be willing to be flexible in what you ask for. Do your homework through the human resources department before you ask.

Item	"STOP" (Red)	"CAUTION" (Yellow)	"Proceed" (Green)
Accelerated performance review with a bonus attached.	✓		

Tactics when discussing:
You might need to compromise on a bonus. If they have other forms of reward, such as conference attendance or time off, work with the employer.

Item	"STOP" (Red)	"CAUTION" (Yellow)	"Proceed" (Green)
Hiring bonus.		✓	

Tactics when discussing:
Some employers use a hiring bonus as a standard practice and some do not. Do your homework on the employer (maybe through a recruiter) before you ask for this.

Now it is your turn to identify your own issues. Where do they fall on the confrontation spectrum and what tactics can you use to address them?

CONFRONTATION SPECTRUM

	"STOP" (Red)	"CAUTION" (Yellow)	"Proceed" (Green)
Item: _____	_____	_____	_____
Tactics when discussing:			
Item: _____	_____	_____	_____
Tactics when discussing:			
Item: _____	_____	_____	_____
Tactics when discussing:			
Item: _____	_____	_____	_____
Tactics when discussing:			
Item: _____	_____	_____	_____
Tactics when discussing:			
Item: _____	_____	_____	_____
Tactics when discussing:			
Item: _____	_____	_____	_____
Tactics when discussing:			

This is a good place to refer back to the negotiation profiles in Chapter 11. Sensitize yourself to your blind spots and use the confrontation spectrum to proactively develop tactics for discussing the tough issues.

Good communication and rapport do not just happen during a negotiated exchange. They are the result of preparation and keen awareness of the dynamics between you and the employer. If you have good communication and rapport, don't take them for granted. If you are working on these aspects of your relationship with the employer, use the following guidelines as well as the action steps at the end of this chapter to cultivate good communication and rapport.

Communication and Rapport . . . How to Make It Happen

- Listen attentively (quiet the nervous chatter in your head).
- Maintain good eye contact and be calm and composed.
- Be prepared for the exchange so that you are not preoccupied with "if only I had done more homework"! Know what you want.
- Show respect for the other person. Do not interrupt.
- Focus on ways to reinforce connection or collegiality through a sincere compliment.
- Try to see things from the other person's perspective.
- Withhold opinions and judgments until you have heard everything the other person has to say.
- Avoid a response until you are sure that you know and understand what the other person means.
- Mirror back what you have heard and confirm your understanding.

Action Items

**Check
When
Completed**

_____ Recognize the milestone of receiving the offer.

_____ Review your negotiation profile in Chapter 11
and plan for a difference of opinion.

_____ Work with the confrontation zones *(red, yellow,
and green).*

_____ Complete the *Confrontation Spectrum* for your
items.

_____ Read the closing guidelines for optimal
communication and rapport.

*The right word may be effective, but no word was ever as
effective as a rightly timed pause.*

MARK TWAIN (SAMUEL L. CLEMENS)

Agenda

- Understanding the four dimensions of communication.

- "Are You a Good, Fair, or Poor Listener?"

- Ten critical questions for checking listening skills and assumptions.

- Sam's Story *(a strong professional team leader compromises on the finer points of an offer).*

A sudden silence in the middle of a conversation suddenly brings us back to essentials: it reveals how dearly we must pay for the invention of speech.

E. M. CIOVAN, 1911–1995
RUMANIAN-BORN FRENCH PHILOSOPHER
CASSELL DICTIONARY OF CONTEMPORARY QUOTATIONS,
ROBERT ANDREWS, 1996, P. 102,
LONDON: CASSELL, WELLINGTON HOUSE

Under *normal* daily circumstances, it is challenging to be a good listener. Busy chatter runs through your mind even when you think you are listening to someone. It takes more energy and self-discipline to listen with undivided attention than it does to express yourself.

Under *unusual* circumstances, such as when you must evaluate and negotiate something personal, like a job offer, it is particularly difficult to concentrate on what someone else is saying.

Communication takes place in four different dimensions: (1) verbal/auditory exchange of information; (2) visual exchange *(e.g., body language)* of messages; (3) tactile exchange *(e.g., handshake)* of messages, and (4) visceral exchange of information:

① *Verbal/auditory.* This refers to the tone used when expressing ideas; the use of inflection; and the language used during the exchange. When we are listening, 38 percent of what we perceive is based on tone and diction; the words themselves provide only 7 percent.

② *Visual (body language).* Is the person comfortable and relaxed, or uncomfortable and tense? According to Sandler Systems, Inc., 1993, when we are communicating in person, 55 percent of what we perceive is visual and directly influenced by body language.

③ *Tactile exchange.* You can glean a great deal of information through a handshake. The way you are greeted can provide good information about how receptive the other person is.

④ *Visceral.* Instinctive, emotional reactions affect all communication. During every exchange, a silent "extra sense" is processing information. We put the cues together from:

What we hear.

What we see.

What we feel.

The result is a series of either positive or negative impressions. The saying that people use when interviewing, "You never have a second chance to make a first impression" is potent. We are often unaware of how much information we are picking up, but we constantly form impressions.

Given the flood of stimuli, good listening is not to be taken for granted. Use the following questions to gauge your ability to listen:

ARE YOU A GOOD, FAIR, OR POOR LISTENER?

① How long are you able to pay attention to what someone is saying before you want to interrupt the person?

☐ 3 minutes ☐ 5 minutes ☐ 10 minutes ☐ 15 minutes ☐ More

② What do you find happens if you do not respond after 5 minutes? Do you begin a rebuttal in your mind?

☐ Yes ☐ No

③ What kind of emotional response interferes with your ability to listen?

☐ Anxiety ☐ Joy ☐ Nervousness ☐ Other?

Now assess your responses. On *Question 1,* unless you checked the "More" box, you are not as active a listener as you probably think! This chapter will help you pinpoint the circumstances in which you have the greatest trouble listening—and offer some practical remedies!

On *Question 2,* if you answered "Yes," Watch Out! and read on.

For *Question 3,* there is not a right or wrong answer, but these emotional responses could rob you of your full ability to actively listen. Notice where you get stumped and apply this self-knowledge in the following fill-in exercise.

Be open and listen for the employer's meaning. This is extremely important. When tension in a negotiation interferes with a good exchange of information, you or the employer need to *stop* to get the communication back on track.

Subtle as this part of the process is, *you* need to work through the following questions to become clear about your ability to handle this dimension.

BEING A GOOD LISTENER

Consider These First

① *What might interfere with my ability to listen? What might distract me* (e.g., my emotions; my determination and desire to arrive at a specific outcome; intimidation about the process because it is unfamiliar)? Please elaborate.

_____

_____

_____

_____

② *When do I listen to others most effectively and how can I replicate this skill in this situation?* Please elaborate.

_____

_____

_____

_____

Consider the Offer at Hand

③ *What concerns do I need to be aware of and plan for?* Please elaborate.

_____

_____

_____

④ *How can I make sure I understand the message and the intent of the employer during the negotiation?* Please elaborate.

_____

_____

_____

_____

⑤ *Are there emotional reactions (defensiveness?) that might arise and potentially diminish my ability to manage my part of the negotiation?* Please elaborate.

_____

_____

_____

_____

⑥ *What assumptions do I have about the employer, about the company, and about the hiring and negotiation process* (e.g., they are unwilling to bend or change. . . they do not want to deviate from what they have come up with. . . they are potentially offended by my request to consider making some changes to the package. . . they are more powerful than I am, and I could quickly and easily be in a very uncomfortable position)? Please elaborate.

_____

_____

_____

⑦ *Which assumptions are probably correct?* Please elaborate.

_____

_____

_____

_____

⑧ *Which assumptions are possibly incorrect?* Please elaborate.

_____

_____

_____

_____

⑨ *What questions could I pose that would allow me to check my as-sumptions about them and about the negotiation process* (e.g., in what areas does flexibility exist? What is of critical importance to them and why? In previous hires, how would they character-ize or describe a successful resolution of issues involving the terms of agreement? In what ways could we address important is-sues— face-to-face meetings are always preferable— and who might need to be involved at this stage in the process)? Please elaborate.

_____

_____

_____

_____

⑩ *What are the important details in this process?* Why (e.g., maintain *healthy control of your emotions* so that you can listen intently and not be internally conflicted; make sure to *ask questions* before operating on assumption; remember to *state the positives* in the situation *before* you talk about the challenging issues)? Please elaborate.

_____

_____

_____

_____

Consider Sam's experience as you think about the details of the offer:

SAM'S STORY

Sam was being recruited for a newly defined role in the company. A combination of management, finance, and information systems would rest under his leadership. The company recruiting him recognized Sam's talent for cross-functional leadership and wanted him to spearhead a major project.

The five-month-long interview process was protracted, but the interest remained strong for both parties. Sam knew that the match between his skills and the requirements of the position was good and he expected to get a job offer.

The offer finally came through at the end of five months and Sam reviewed the details of the package. Three aspects of the offer presented concerns for him:

① His medical benefit was not going to be covered 100 percent by the company.

② His salary was not going to make up for the difference in medical coverage.

③ The profit-sharing plan that he had with his former employer was far superior to that of the plan with this company.

Sam engaged in a face-to-face negotiation with the employer and the following dialogue played out:

Employer: Sam, thank you for coming in. We hope that you are satisfied with the offer.

Sam: Good morning. A substantial part of the package looks good. I do have a few areas of concern. *(Sam's body language [visual] is relaxed and confident.)*

Employer: Can you give me some details?

Sam: Yes. The healthcare plan you have is less comprehensive in dollar coverage than the plan I currently have. *(Sam answers questions quickly and directly [verbal/auditory].)*

Employer: Sam, I'm sorry, but as much as I would like to be able to change that, we can't adjust that part of the package.

Sam: It sounds as if you are locked into a companywide plan that lends itself to little, if any, flexibility. *(Watch Out! defensiveness starts to creep into Sam's language.)*

Employer: You're right. What else about the offer needs attention?

Sam: Given the out-of-pocket difference between what I am currently receiving in benefits and what your healthcare plan is, I would like to look for a way to close the gap. Probably salary would be the best part of the offer to work with. *(Sam recovers—tone and words are more open and flexible.)*

Employer: Can you suggest an amount for an increase in salary?

Sam: Yes, between a 5 percent and 10 percent increase in base compensation.

Employer: I don't think we could reach the 10 percent level, but we could work with a 5–6 percent increase in base compensation.

> **What do YOU observe in the rest of the dialogue?**

Sam: That would be good. I have calculated the numbers and I would be fine with that.

Employer: Good. You said that you had a few areas. Are there remaining items that need attention?

Sam: Yes. The profit-sharing plan I currently have is substantially more lucrative than the plan you have. I am concerned about the net effect of that on my overall earnings and would appreciate your addressing this.

Employer: Sam, we can't do anything with the profit-sharing plan. What would you suggest we do?

Sam: Are there areas of flexibility in any other part of the package?

Employer: Well, we could increase your year-end bonus. If we incorporate a 6 percent increase in base salary, the value of the bonus will also reflect this increase. We could add 5 percent more to that year-end bonus and attempt to close the gap represented in the difference between profit-sharing plans. Would that work for you?

Sam: Yes, that would work for me. Thank you.

Employer: Sam, we look forward to having you on board.

Sam: I am also. Thanks again for adjusting these aspects of the offer. Will these changes be represented in a revised offer letter?

Employer: Yes, I will get it to you within the next couple of days.

Sam: I look forward to getting this phase of my transition completed and look forward to working here.

Sam did not get everything he wanted, but he got the majority of what he asked for. He had to exercise self-discipline when the employer responded without flexibility to the healthcare plan. Sam noticed his *defenses* creeping into his attitude and had to quickly *neutralize* them in order to concentrate on the rest of the exchange.

He used a couple of mental reminders to get himself focused: *Stay focused on the salary and profit plan* and *take a deep breath and relax.* His strategy for catching himself, as he felt defenses coming up, involved calming himself down and refocusing—similar to the habits Olympic athletes develop to stay in control of themselves and their performance. The process of mental imaging and suggestion is powerful and effective.

At the first sign of resistance from the employer, Sam could have assumed that the employer was not going to exercise good faith effort and was uncooperative. Instead, by assuming that there was good faith effort and that the negotiation was worthwhile, Sam made progress and realized some difference in the package.

Action Items

**Check
When
Completed**

_____ Complete the *Are You a Good, Fair, or Poor Listener?* quiz.

_____ Highlight the information about the four dimensions of communication: verbal, visual, tactile, and visceral.

_____ Answer the 10 questions listed under *Being a Good Listener.*

_____ Review the descriptions of *negotiation profiles* (Chapter 11) and strategize around how, given your profile, you can exercise good listening skills.

_____ Read Sam's Story and notice what you observe about his listening skills.

I could never make out what those damned dots meant.

LORD RANDOLPH CHURCHILL
FORMER CHANCELLOR OF THE EXCHEQUER
(REGARDING DECIMAL POINTS)

Manage Your Language, Tone, and Demeanor

Agenda

- Appraise how you express yourself in most situations.

- Critique how you use language, tone, and demeanor when you are trying to get a point across.

- Develop a plan to minimize your communication weaknesses and maximize your communication strengths.

- Nancy's Story *(a senior technical manager with an MBA strikes a strong deal).*

- Enlist constructive feedback.

A word is not a crystal, transparent and unchanging, it is the skin of a living thought and may vary greatly in color and content according to the circumstances and time in which it is used.

OLIVER WENDELL HOLMES, JR., OPINION
TOWNE V. EISNER, JANUARY 7, 1918

Date: Today

To: All Negotiators Who Want to Perfect Their
           Communication Skills

Subject: The Invincible Triangle: Language, Tone, and Demeanor

---

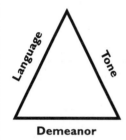

Picture a triangle with three equally important sides—no matter which way you flip it, one leg cannot stand without the other two. Peak communication in negotiating is like that—it consists of three equally critical components: Language *(the actual words you speak);* Tone *(the modulation and expression of your voice in speaking these words);* and Demeanor *(the non-verbal expression and nuances that powerfully communicate your overall presence in any verbal exchange).* Good negotiators master all three legs of the triangle.

Without language and tone, it would be hard to get a sense of demeanor or style of communication. The three aspects of communication in concert are what characterize the atmosphere of an interaction or exchange. The atmosphere is important.

Separate out these three components of expression and reflect on how you express yourself, and you will find this dimension of the negotiation more manageable.

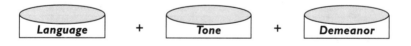

Use the chart on page 152 to work through the three platforms for effective communication. Identify answers to the *example* questions and plan follow-through steps. Use the form provided.

Preparation	Follow-Through Strategy
Tone *When do I express enthusiasm?* *Is it natural?* **Sample Response:** When I feel excited about a challenge and about the people. **Your Response:**	In my discussion, concentrate on the parts of the opportunity that are most exciting.
Demeanor *What does my body language reveal about my level of comfort or discomfort?* **Sample Response:** If I'm not careful, I seem awkward and aloof. **Your Response:**	Think about the parts of the interview when I felt most connected with the person.

Now that you have answered these questions, use the following chart to create responses for each category.

Preparation	Follow-Through Strategy
Language ① *How well do I use language to get my point across? Do I provide enough detail and data?* **Your Response:** _[handwritten]_	① _[handwritten]_
② *When someone communicates differently than I do, how do I bridge the gap to try to establish greater understanding?* **Your Response:** _[handwritten]_	② _[handwritten]_
③ *How comfortable am I with verbal communication?* **Your Response:** _[handwritten]_	③
	(continued)

Preparation	Follow-Through Strategy
Tone	
① When do I express enthusiasm? Is it natural?	①
Your Response: _____	
② When do I express energy? Is it natural?	②
Your Response: _____	
Demeanor	
① What does my body language reveal about my level of comfort or discomfort?	①
Your Response: _____	
② Who can give me honest, constructive feedback about how I communicate in different situations?	②
Your Response: _____	

NANCY'S STORY

Nancy, an MBA and a professional engineer with over 20 years of experience, worked in a large, high-tech manufacturing plant. She had recently gone through a reengineering and merger situation and was being recruited for four different positions. Three of the four would have involved relocation and after several phone interviews and at least one "in-person" interview at each location, she decided to pursue the local opportunity.

Because Nancy wanted to maximize her chances of getting an offer that worked for her on many levels, she embarked on a soul-searching exercise to assess and better utilize her personal communication style. Before she began, she assessed the situation as objectively as she could:

The local Chief Operating Officer opportunity with a medium-size, high-tech manufacturing company was very attractive. The challenges involved in the position, the proximity of the organization to where she lived, and the industry were of great interest to her. As she entered the final interview, she realized some discrepancy between what she wanted in an offer package and what they were going to offer. She also reflected on her concerns about the offer and how she might react. In addition, she had received a lot of feedback about her communication style from former colleagues.

Disappointed in the bonus plan, stock options, and exit support part of the offer, she isolated the numbers and justification needed to close the gap. After the calculations were done, she focused on the character dimension of the people she was considering joining up with. Part of her assessment of the people was her estimation of *their* motivation to work out the right kind of package.

Being objective about herself was the next challenge. She had valuable feedback from her colleagues about her work style and style of interaction. Without this feedback, an honest self-appraisal would have been difficult. With it, she was able to work with specific data and develop her communication strategy. Narrowing the gap with some degree of confidence was going to take a great deal of careful planning. Reflecting on the feedback was difficult, but the truthful information proved fruitful.

Nancy approached her *Personal Communication Critique* by dissecting each of the three legs of the triangle: Language, Tone, and Demeanor. The order in which she tackled each area was less important than getting down her raw thoughts on the ways she communicated in each dimension currently, and how she might correct and improve them.

NANCY'S PERSONAL COMMUNICATION CRITIQUE

Area of Improvement	Corrective Strategy
Language In her verbal and written communication, she was "stilted and impersonal."	She deliberately selected words and phrases that would invite a cooperative response. She also began each point with a positive statement (*Good morning, how are you?* or *Thank you for the way you handled . . .*).
Tone **Too Stiff** In interpersonal interactions in the workplace, she was too "stiff," too "autocratic," and too "removed" from the people.	She decided to concentrate on the constructive, positive qualities in the other person and begin the exchange with attention to these qualities (*e.g., hobbies in common, item in the news of interest to the employer*).
Demeanor **Too Rigid and Formal** In the structuring of work, she was "too rigid and formal." The message relayed by the overtly tight hold on the work and the organization was that she did not trust anyone.	She established some ground rules for herself. She would use this negotiation to loosen up her style of communication. She noted the constructive, positive aspects of the interviews and concentrated on the positive rapport that had begun to form.
Somber She was regarded with extreme caution by her colleagues because she held everyone under intense scrutiny and had very low tolerance for mistakes. People were afraid to open up in meetings. She had a sobering and somber effect on the entire organization.	She paid close attention to relaxing her push for perfection. She recognized how much that played a role in everything she did and how it made for strained interactions (*she saw a connection between her tendency to expect perfection from everyone and the resulting tension and strain in the atmosphere of the workplace*). By diminishing her need for perfection, she could begin to pay more attention to the interpersonal relationship aspects of her interaction with the employer.

After completing her honest evaluation, Nancy was now ready to blaze ahead with newfound insights and self-confidence. Her meeting was in person, and some aspects of the negotiation looked like this:

Nancy: Hi, Steve. Thank you for the meeting. It's been very exciting to get to know the inner workings of this organization. I appreciate the level of professionalism I've observed in all areas.

Steve: Thank you, Nancy. It's good to see you again. We've looked for the right person for a long time, and it hasn't been easy to find someone. We're pleased to have identified you as a good match for this position.

Nancy: It must have been challenging to go through the interview process for the COO position. Your work is in such a specialized niche of the high-tech industry.

Steve: Well Nancy, what do we need to do next?

Nancy: Steve, the base compensation for the position is good and the benefits are good. My fact finding shows me that you have designed a good combination of items. However, I do have concerns with three parts of the package.

Steve: Can you elaborate on the three areas that don't meet your expectations?

Nancy: Yes. First, I know how unpredictable this industry can be, and though I am interested and eager to join your organization, I would like an exit plan and severance package to be included in this offer.

Steve: Nancy, you are right to bring this up. We have been so invested in the building part of our business that, frankly, we have not included a contingency clause for exit support. We will gladly include that. Would you draw up some categories you would want included and some dollar ranges for each category?

Nancy: Yes. I could get that to you within the next couple of days.

Steve: What else is of concern to you?

Nancy: Steve, the bonus plan is conservatively constructed. May I ask what was factored into the plan?

Steve: Yes. We have taken annual net earnings, factored in the adjustment for inflation and projected out a percentage of what we need to reinvest in the business and then looked at a bonus distribution that would reflect parity for everyone in the organization.

Nancy: Thank you for outlining the process. I suggest that you incorporate a differential for the key roles in the company. This is one of those roles because the stability, viability, and strategic direction of the organization are directly and significantly impacted by this position.

Steve: We will take this under consideration. I will have to go back to my Board of Directors to work on this issue. Our next Board meeting is at the end of next week.

Nancy: Thank you. I respect the value of parity in this organization, but I also think that greater risk and responsibility for the health and progression of the organization rest with the individuals in certain roles. The bonus plan does not reflect the disparate way in which risk is distributed in the organization.

Steve: *(Notice momentum and flow of the conversation.)* I can appreciate your comments. I will get back with you on this after the next Board meeting. I can't promise anything, but I will do my best to incorporate an increase. Is there another area of concern that we need to work with?

Nancy: *(Notice tone.)* Yes. First, thank you for taking the bonus allocation portion of the offer package under consideration and for presenting it before the Board.

Steve: You're welcome. Certainly.

Nancy: The last item of concern involves the stock options. I am interested in a greater investment on your part in the initial numbers of shares.

Steve: Why do you feel this way?

Nancy: Because I am of the conviction that based on my track record, I will make contributions to the value and profit of the company equal to that level of initial shares of stock.

Steve: Can you tell me more? We've never done this for anyone before.

Nancy: The package I had with my former company involved 15% more options valued at the amount that I am suggesting we establish. This level resulted from two annual performance appraisals and calculations that correlated corporate earnings with my contributions.

Steve: That's intriguing and valid. I will have to take this under consideration with my Board. Again, I cannot promise anything, but I can present this and maybe the number of shares over a two-year time frame can be increased.

Nancy: Thank you. I want to respect your guidelines, but I also value the impact that higher initial offerings make.

Steve: We value your background and track record, and we think there is a good match between your capabilities and experience and what we need.

Nancy: Thank you. Can we meet again after the Board Meeting?

Steve: Yes, and I will look forward to your letter outlining the exit support categories and ranges.

Nancy and Steve reconciled and resolved two-thirds of the areas that represented discrepancies. The Board approved an exit support package with one year of pay and transition support/outplacement support. They also increased the initial contribution of shares of stock.

They did not adjust the bonus plan and indicated that what might have been included in the bonus plan would be reflected in the increase in the number of shares of stock incorporated in the offer. Their reasoning for not altering the bonus was that they wanted to ensure a fair distribution across the organization, and the morale of employees was too directly linked to the bonus plan to alter it.

Nancy has done well in the organization. In the two years that have passed since she joined the team, she has performed effectively and the company has benefited from her contributions.

The circumspect way in which she evaluated herself proved helpful. She engendered such a high degree of comfort and confidence in herself during the preparation that she was able to extend that into the final stage of negotiation.

Not only did her efforts close the gap between what she wanted and what they offered, but she was formally included in a succession plan to become the next president of the company.

Describe your strengths when you communicate: _____

_____

_____

_____

_____

_____

_____

Outline your ideas for improving your communication style:

1. _____

_____

_____

2. _____

_____

_____

3. _____

_____

_____

4. _____

_____

_____

Action Items

**Check
When
Completed**

_____ Conduct a *Personal Communication Critique.*

_____ Design and implement a communication improvement plan *(e.g., join a Toastmasters Club).*

_____ Conduct and critique a videotaped presentation.

_____ Enlist feedback about your verbal communication style from a respected colleague or friend.

_____ Evaluate your negotiating style *(from Chapter 11)* and plan for the possible pitfalls.

_____ Recognize your verbal communication strengths and capitalize on them by incorporating them in your negotiation approach.

Language is the soul of intellect, and reading is the essential process by which that intellect is cultivated beyond the commonplace experiences of everyday life.

CHARLES SCRIBNER, JR.
PUBLISHERS WEEKLY, MARCH 30, 1984

CHAPTER 16

Present Concerns
with Clarity and
Factual Information

Agenda

- Using facts to present a winning formula.

- Some important questions.

- Where to go to get the facts.

- Comparing fact based/professional tone and subjective/personal tone.

- Staying savvy with the facts: Completing a budget.

We think in generalities, but we live in detail.

ALFRED NORTH WHITEHEAD

Date: Today

To: Negotiators Who Need to Be Armed with the Facts

Subject: How to Communicate Concerns with Clarity
           and Objectivity

During a negotiation, grounding yourself in the facts equips you to handle the most tension-filled interactions. *The facts serve as a bridge* between what you want and what the employer wants. They can help neutralize a tense situation and can be the tool you need in discussing difficult issues.

In your dealings with the employer, use facts to convey your most important points. First, clarify your *concern* and *state* it in as neutral and professional way as possible. Next, provide supporting facts and, finally, give examples to illustrate your statement of concern.

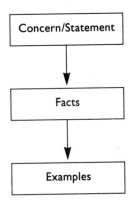

Your Concern: The relocation package being proposed by the employer does not meet your expectations and/or your needs.

Statement: I have some concerns about the proposed relocation package.

Facts: According to an industry survey of top 100 employers (have survey with you), most companies do include up to six months of temporary living expenses for the new employee at this position level. In addition, an informal polling of recruiters specialized in this industry (say hospital administration) informed me that temporary living expenses are almost uniformly covered by leading employers in our field.

Example: Cite one or two specific firms based on the preceding research as benchmarks.

Answers to the following questions will serve you well:

What are the best sources for factual information about my field?

Use your professional association representative or a good reference librarian. When approaching a reference librarian, ask for assistance in the following way:

You: Hi. I am considering an offer of employment and want to gather some data about salary and benefits in my field. Can you tell me where I should go to find this information? Are there reference sources, journals, or periodicals I should consult?

Reference Librarian: Yes, there are several resources available for that kind of information. Can you tell me more about your professional field?

You: Yes, I have a background in _____ and have training and credentials in _____. I have worked in the _____ industry and am considering an offer in the _____ industry.

Is there anyone in particular I should contact?

Yes. Someone who is in retained or executive search, or the president of your professional association, or the association for the field you want to go into (refer to Chapter 12).

What do I need to know about my fair market value that will allow me to speak with businesslike conviction?

Refer back to Chapter 6 for a checklist of what you need to know to evaluate your professional worth.

Where can I get information about salaries, benefits, vacation time, performance review process, training and development, and amount of travel required in comparable positions?

For salaries, use *The National Business Employment Weekly.* Use a salary survey from your professional association. The chart on page 166 suggests resources for all these areas of interest.

How can I present this information so that it is accepted as factual and research-based rather than as an intimidation tactic?

Fact Based/Professional Tone *Reactions and Phrasing That Work Well*	Subjective/Personal Tone *Reactions and Phrasing to Avoid*
Vacation Time Thank you for the offer. Several aspects of the offer are very appealing. However, in the area of vacation, my homework among colleagues at this level, a few representatives from retained search firms, and my professional society journal indicate that two to three weeks vacation is more the norm. Can we discuss ways to adjust the one-week vacation time in this package?	Thank you for the offer. Most of what is in the package is fine, but I have always had a two-week vacation. I would like to have two weeks off if I come to work for you. How can we do this?
Salary I can appreciate the process you probably followed to put this package together. I would like to share with you some homework I have done. I have researched the fair market value for my experience and functional expertise and have found the average salary in this field to be 20% higher than what is in this offer. In what area is there flexibility?	I make $X now and would prefer not to slide backward in my earning potential.

WHERE TO GO TO GET THE FACTS

Topic	Library (Reference)	Professional Association	Alma Mater/ Alumni Association	Retained or Contingency Search Firm	National Business Employment Weekly	Real Estate
Salaries	☺	☺	☺	☺	☺	
Benefits	☺	☺		☺		
Vacation Time		☺		☺		
Performance Review Process		☺		☺		
Training and Development	☺	☺				
Amount of Travel Required		☺		☺	☺	
Cost-of-Living Information	☺			☺	☺	☺

How often has this person with whom I am dealing been engaged in negotiations about job offers and what has resulted from those efforts?

Ask your contact person, "How common has it been for candidates to negotiate?" "Have you brought anyone else into this process?" If so, "Why?" If not, "Why not?"

How readily might they accept my research and my approach?

This will depend on three factors:

① How thoroughly you have done your homework.
② Your tone of voice and demeanor while you are presenting the information.
③ Your focus on common interests.

Remember: Concentrate on common interests that involve goals you and the employer share. These might be:

• Maintaining or improving the relationship.
• Arriving at a set of terms which are satisfactory for both parties.
• Resolving differences and cultivating positive momentum.

Being savvy with facts involves the following:

① Do your financial forecasting:
   a. Know your market value *(refer to Chapter 6).*
   b. Complete a budget *(a sample budget follows).*   .

What Do You Need?
($ per Month)

Housing	_____
Utilities	_____
Food	_____
Clothing	_____

Transportation   _____

Insurance   _____

Healthcare   _____

Child Care or Elder Care   _____

Taxes   _____

Entertainment   _____

Savings   _____

   TOTAL $ _____

    c. Create a range ($45–60K, $50–65K, etc.) to avoid locking yourself into one number.

② Write phrases that will help you avoid stating a figure first. *(Refer to Chapter 10.)*

③ Remember to balance the relationship with the facts.

④ Concern yourself with common interests.

⑤ Stay clearheaded!

Good Luck!

Action Items

**Check
When
Completed**

_____ Develop your points using the statement of concern, facts, and example formula.

_____ Answer the questions in the chapter.

_____ Study the chart *Where to Go to Get the Facts.*

_____ Use the comparison chart.

_____ Complete a budget worksheet based on the sample budget provided.

I do not feel obligated to believe that the same God who has endowed us with sense, reason, and intellect has intended us to forgo their use.

GALILEO GALILEI

<table>
<tr><td></td><td>*Incorporate Flexibility, Compromise, and Alternatives in Your Strategy*</td></tr>
</table>

Agenda

- Planning as the answer to Winging It.

- Analyzing reminders and goals in the process, relationship, and strategy areas of negotiation.

- Laura's Story (a senior-level administrator compromises and comes out ahead).

- Compromise and "What Went Right."

- Trade-offs and script.

- Six important questions.

Every great mistake has a halfway moment, a split second when it can be recalled and perhaps remedied.

PEARL S. BUCK
WHAT AMERICA MEANS TO ME, 1942

Date: Today

To: Everyone Willing to Create Compromise and Alternatives to Come Out Ahead

Subject: *Planning* for Flexibility in the Negotiation Process

---

Backing yourself into a corner happens quickly and, at times, mysteriously. Preventing the rigid, frozen response *is* possible. If you feel yourself freeze up as you engage in the discussion, this is your cue that flexibility is needed. The key to thawing out in the negotiation process can be summarized in one work: *Planning.*

Watch Out! Don't wing it—Your wings will be clipped early on in the process!

Planning entails not only carefully outlining your own objectives, creative ways to reach them, and areas where you can bend to achieve the end, but also anticipating the employer's response in every scenario that you can imagine. The mistake that many negotiators make is not taking the time to fully comprehend—and articulate, at least to themselves—the employer's perspective.

It is important to use several of the following steps.

First, step back from the temptation to get a quick result and, instead, *focus on the process and the relationship.* If you are involved in a lengthy discussion, use reminder points on a sheet of paper. When under pressure, you are likely to forget important points. A reminder list could look something like this:

SAMPLE PROCESS REMINDERS

Goals

① Work on agreement about vacation time. *I could settle for 1½– 2 weeks.*

② Discuss ways to substitute their medical benefits for more base compensation. *I have medical benefits through my partner's health plan. That will give me and the employer flexibility.*

③ Examine a flexible work schedule. *I could be on call or available five days a week but in the office four days.*

④ Discuss adjusting the start date.

SAMPLE RELATIONSHIP REMINDERS

Goals

① Reassure them that I am very interested in the organization and the opportunity.

② Review and confirm ways in which I could address and solve major problems they are facing.

③ Verbally appreciate the ways in which I have been treated throughout the interview process.

④ Indicate that I can appreciate their desire to settle on the terms of agreement. *I recognize that they, like me, have been involved in this process for a while.*

SAMPLE STRATEGY REMINDERS

Goals

① To establish areas that we are both interested in and to use that as the foundation for the discussion. For example:

They want me to begin resolving issues, and I want to begin working.

They want to make sure that when I start working for them, I feel that I have been treated well. I want them to feel confident that the way I have conducted myself in this negotiation is the way I would conduct myself on behalf of the organization—fairly and intelligently.

② To show that I am choosing to engage in this discussion for the right reasons—out of respect for my skills and value.

Increasing flexibility in a negotiation involves stepping back from the details and looking at the overall objectives and the bigger picture of what is happening. If you are fiercely pursuing one set of outcomes *(such as a rigidly set 20 percent increase in base salary, three weeks of vacation, an office with windows, and a bonus)*, rather than looking at a set of priorities and working with an attitude of *compromise,* you will find yourself locked into a corner.

What does compromise look like and why is it important?

Compromise is different for each person. It is a dynamic interchange between parties whose goal is to reach a final agreement but who are facing some strongly held interests and some real possibility for dissension and conflict. Compromise is important because both parties have to feel that they are gaining more than they are giving up.

When you are facing the person who has tendered an offer, the *last* thing you want is to create unnecessary conflict. Disagreement does not automatically translate into conflict.

Remember, the three keys to successful compromise are:

① *Use the planning process to think through specific avenues before you enter the discussion.*

② *Reinforce and acknowledge the quality of the relationship and rapport built to date.*

③ *Stay strategic—keep a clear view of the bigger picture at all times.*

Laura's Story is a strong example of a well-planned compromise situation.

LAURA'S STORY

Laura was a talented senior-level administrator. Her skills on the job were complemented by her strong sense of motivation and willingness to be of service in a high people contact environment. The pace of work was very fast, and as she evaluated her performance, she decided that she wanted to ask for a bonus and a base salary increase.

Laura realized that she would have to incorporate some kind of justification for the salary increase that would be based on her accomplishments and proven talents. The areas of compromise were:

- She would take a bonus over a salary increase.
- She would work toward a bonus and salary increase over time, if she and the employer could agree on a timetable and a set of performance outcomes.
- She would trade off a bonus for a change in title, if a salary increase was also attached.
- She would assume more areas of accountability, if she could get a salary increase.

Step 1. *In preparation for discussing her priorities, Laura outlined some anticipated concerns her manager might have:*

Employer's Concerns

① Want to ensure internal pay equity.

② Want to allow for growth and increase in pay in six months.

③ Want to encourage and provide incentives for the appropriate kinds of skills, work behaviors, motivations, and outcomes.

Step 2. *Next, she outlined her capabilities and qualities that had made her a strong contributor in her career:*

Laura's Capabilities

① Proactive and responsive to all needs within the organization.

② Professional, consistent, and highly skilled in all core functional areas in the organization.

③ Eager to learn, contribute, and maintain high standards.

④ Flexible, "can-do" attitude.

⑤ Self-directed and multiskilled.

Step 3. *Next, Laura planned a script to rehearse. She did not plan to take this into her negotiation, but she used it to ground herself in a basic outline of thought.*

Sample Script: I can appreciate what we have to accomplish. The work is very important and requires full dedication and skill. In the past couple of months, I have made the level of contribution which I think has made a difference. In light of that, I think an increase in salary is warranted. In light of having done the work of two people, I would appreciate an increase as soon as possible. I have outlined five areas of capability and contribution that have made a difference on our team in the past couple of months. If we need to talk about what the budget would or would not allow for, I would like to do that.

Step 4. *Next, Laura outlined for herself the areas of trade-off:*

Laura's Trade Offs

① She would take a bonus over a salary increase.

② She would be willing to work toward a bonus and salary increase over time, if she and the employer could agree on a timetable and a set of performance outcomes.

③ She would trade off a bonus for a change in title, if she could get a salary increase.

④ She would assume more areas of accountability, if she could get a salary increase.

These four trade-offs allowed Laura and the employer to be more flexible and creative in arriving at a workable outcome.

Laura ended up discussing her priorities over the course of two meetings. As some tension began to creep into the first discussion, she asked that they reconvene at a later hour in the day, if possible. When they resumed their discussion, the objectivity they were able to bring to the exchange allowed them to arrive at some final terms of the agreement.

They agreed to a two-month timetable with specific performance objectives, a 10 percent increase in salary, and a corresponding change in title if the objectives were reached. The process worked well for both parties.

What went right here?

- Laura did not enter the discussion fixed on a single outcome—in this case, a salary increase and a bonus. She spent a good deal of preparation time focused on anticipating the employer's likely priorities and needs.

Take Note! Always think through the employer's perspective when planning for compromise scenarios. *(Work through the information and exercises in Chapter 5.)*

- Laura initiated dividing the discussion between two meetings. It was easier for both parties to save face and think more objectively about alternatives and options.

  Be willing to ask for an opportunity to come back to the negotiation if it begins to be heated.

- Laura never backed herself into a corner. She came into the discussion armed with multiple trade-off possibilities.

  Use your creativity—think through *many* acceptable outcomes so that you *win* in every possible negotiation scenario.

Use the following questions to organize your thinking and plan for incorporating flexibility, compromise, and alternatives:

SIX IMPORTANT QUESTIONS

① Where am I likely to be frustrated or bogged down in the negotiation process?

② How can I avoid this kind of reaction and maintain a flexible, constructive attitude?

③ In what ways can I prepare myself for reasonable compromise?

④ What might they bring up that could require my need to compromise?

⑤ How can I generate the greatest number of alternatives so that they do not feel they are being backed into a corner but will allow me to get some of what I want?

⑥ How will I ask for more time or another meeting if we get bogged down?

Flexibility and compromise result from planning. It will pay off for you! Take a few minutes to capture your answers to the Six Important Questions.

List your areas of trade-offs:

1. _____
   _____

2. _____
   _____

3. _____
   _____

4. _____
   _____

5. _____
   _____

6. _____
   _____

7. _____
   _____

Action Items

**Check
When
Completed**

_____ Go over the reminders and goals for the
dimensions of the negotiation:

Process.

Relationship.

Strategy.

_____ Read Laura's Story.

_____ Replicate Steps 1 through 4 for your
negotiation.

_____ Outline multiple trade-offs to cultivate
flexibility and compromise.

_____ Develop a brief outline or script to rehearse
before you enter the discussion.

_____ Answer the *Six Important Questions.*

*Controversial proposals, once accepted, soon become
hallowed.*

DEAN ACHESON, SPEECH
INDEPENDENCE, MO, MARCH 31, 1962

Separate the Personal Issues from the Career/Business Issues

Agenda

- Differentiating between personal issues and career/business issues.

- John's Story *(a seasoned executive successfully negotiates for better life balance).*

- Using your knowledge of negotiation profiles to create an effective exchange.

- *Professional Qualifications Chart (exercise).*

Any soldier worth his salt should be antiwar. And still there are things worth fighting for.

GENERAL H. NORMAN SCHWARZKOPF

Date: Today

To: All Effective Negotiators

Subject: Coming Together by Creating a Healthy Divide

How can you successfully separate your personal interests from your career interests? The two areas quickly become intermingled. Extracting business interests from personal issues or motivations requires careful discernment and homework. You will find this part of the process more manageable if you use the exercises in Chapter 1 and Chapter 6. This homework will help you stay more objective as you begin outlining your interests.

What does "personal" interest mean? . . . What does "career/business" interest mean?

Personal interests are those that *do not* relate to market data, while career/business interests *can be* tied to factual information. Examples of interests in each category are:

Personal Interests	Career/Business Interests
Definition:	
• Tied to subjective preferences.	• Tied to objective, numerical, verifiable factors.
• Tied to ego-driven needs.	
• Tied to personal wants.	• Tied to supply/demand dynamics.
	• Tied to professional association salary survey data.
Examples:	
• Big office.	• Base *salary (tied to salary survey information).*
• Support *person (administrative assistant, etc.).*	
• Reduced percentage of travel required.	• Relocation allowance *(based on cost-of-living data for the region).*

Step 1. Becoming objective about your situation requires some special steps. First and foremost, identify areas of *common interest* for you and the employer. *It is from these areas of common interest that the open flow of information will occur in its best form.* Keep asking yourself the question, *"What's in it for both of us?"* John's Story illustrates these dynamics.

JOHN'S STORY

John met all the project expansion position specifications. His experience had been in other industries, but he was a 15-year veteran of the business world and had a very interesting capital project management background. John had worked in two different industries and was interested in making a career change *and* in working ¾ time rather than full-time. He had given everything to his professional life in the past and wanted to establish some balance.

John had quickly become a valued candidate. The hiring manger, the director of manufacturing, and the plant manager saw his background, related industry knowledge, management skills, and personality as a strong match for what they needed. The interviews proceeded well and the members of the selection team were considering John for several roles. They were convinced that regardless of the position, he would perform outstandingly.

During the last series of interviews, John was prepared for a possible offer of employment. His delineation of personal and career/business issues, (and the positive or negative charge associated with the issues) was clear in his mind.

John had done some research on the company through a former colleague who had interviewed with the company in the past couple of years. With that data in hand, he felt reasonably assured of his assessment about which of his priorities they would match and which ones they might not match. He also attempted to gauge how easy (+) or complicated (−) his discussion about each item would be. He put a check (✓) in the negative (−) column if he thought it would be a complicated discussion rife with resistance, as shown in the chart on the top of page 183.

John was sensitive to the complexities of an expansion. He had been involved as a member of an expansion team and as a leader of a team. He knew that there was the sense during an expansion climate that there was too much to accomplish and not enough hours in the day to accomplish it.

JOHN'S ANALYSIS

+	−	Personal
✓		Commuting Well within my desired commuting distance.
	✓	Child care Child care allowance not offered.
	✓	Work Less than Full Time 3/4 time position (will allow me to spend time on other parts of my life).
		Career/Business
✓		Position Project management using my management skills, leadership skills.
✓		Reasonable support from organization (staff, resources, and political support).
	✓	3/4 time position.
✓		Base compensation (stay in line with what I am making or realize a slight increase).
✓		Benefits.

Though everyone at the company liked him and seemed to have the conviction that he was someone they wanted on their team, he knew that an overriding priority for them would be to engage a full-time employee. In anticipation of these concerns being raised, John approached his final interviews with the following strategy:

GOAL: TO REINFORCE THE MATCH BETWEEN WHAT THEY NEED AND WHAT I OFFER

Project Manager Specifications	My Qualifications
7–10 years' related experience.	15 years' related experience.
Project leadership experience.	5 years' project leadership experience.
Bachelor's degree.	Bachelor's Degree.
Advanced degree.	Master's Degree.
Capital improvements experience.	5 years' capital improvements experience.

Areas of common interest for John and the employer:

① *Secure a commitment* (I want them to commit to me as their candidate of choice, *and* they want their top candidate to accept an offer). A great deal of time, energy, and effort has gone into this process.

② *Secure the commitment* while *improving or maintaining a good relationship.* The rapport, camaraderie, and relationship are what will result in strong, positive forward momentum.

③ *Maintain internal equity and morale.* John organized his research and was reminded that few (if any) professionals at his level had ¾ time positions. In addition to that, he could not identify anyone who was involved in a large-scale expansion process who was a part-time professional employee.

John knew that he would have to demonstrate his efficiency and effectiveness in several ways to have any chance of convincing the hiring team that he could contribute at the level they wanted. He used the table on page 185 to depict his vision of important ingredients in the expansion project.

John went into his final interviews and within a day, received an offer of employment; the vote to extend an offer to him was unanimous. John received a telephone call in which the plant manager extended the offer and he received a letter.

John had two subsequent meetings with the plant manager and the hiring manager present. The tables, charts, and background research John had prepared impressed the plant manager and the hiring manager (see chart on page 185). The respective personal and career/business issues were reconciled. The employer agreed to John's ¾ time schedule for three months. At that time, they would conduct a work process and performance review. If John achieved 95 percent of the agreed-on goals (barring any extenuating circumstances and occurrences out of his control), he would be given a go-ahead on continuing to work a ¾ time schedule. If he did not accomplish his goals, he would change his schedule to full time.

The two final discussions were not easy for John. What made the difference was the project table, his research, and his work on outlining the personal issues and career/business issues and identifying the common interests.

John has maintained a ¾ time schedule for nine months, and though the pressure continues, he is making this work. It is his choice to work in this way and he appreciates the company's support. He took a slight cut in base pay, but he has made up for that in the peace of mind associated with having achieved a better balance between his personal and professional lives.

John's Vision: Expansion Plan Project Table

	1st Quarter			2nd Quarter			3rd Quarter	
	Month 1	Month 2	Month 3	Month 4	Month 5	Month 6	Month 7	Month 8
Project Specifications								
Prototype & Revisions								
Budget:								
Outline								
Initial Approval								
Final Parameters								
Final Approval								
Staffing:								
Define Roles								
Project Plan:								
Design								
Testing								
Implement								
						Completed:		
						Experimentation:		
						Ongoing:		

Some examples of common interests for your own situation might include:

- *Solidifying the relationship between you and the company.* Both parties have invested time and energy in pursuing a mutually agreeable relationship. Substantial motivation exists on both sides for a satisfactory outcome.
- *Arriving at a mutually agreed-on set of priorities and terms for the offer.* These include title, responsibilities, reporting relationship(s), formal and functional support, compensation, benefits, and start date.
- *Arriving at a set of expectations for performance results.*
- *Proceeding rather than having to go back to the drawing board to repeat the entire hiring process.*

If you focus on these areas of *common* interest, you will find that items which otherwise might interfere with the flow of discussion can be put into perspective and be handled more expediently. You will not get bogged down in the emotional charge of issues that typically push your buttons.

As you watch for areas of common interest, recognize where your negotiation profiles might differ from that of the employer. *By way of reminder, the four profiles are Wing-It Specialists, Problem Solvers, Adventurers, and Skeptics. Refer back to Chapter 11 for more detail about the four profiles, their qualities, habits, mottoes, traps, and recovery tricks.*

Just as pushing the *pause* button when watching a videotape allows you to "freeze frame" and think about what you have just seen or digest what you have watched, press your *pause* button when you are interacting with the employer. Catch yourself before you get into conflict over a personal or a career/business issue. Negotiation profiles can help you maintain awareness of your style and of the employer's style of negotiation.

It will be your responsibility to sort through your personal and career/business concerns and focus on the career concerns. Once you strategize around these issues and work through the exercises in Chapter 10, you will have to be attuned to the interaction between you and the employer. The interaction will be characterized by the dynamics resulting from your negotiation style and the employer's.

Use the information in Chapter 11 to help you in detecting your style and that of the employer. This awareness will serve as a safety catch for you and will help you insulate yourself from some of the natural emotional reactions.

It is really tough to keep personal issues and career/business issues separate and to assess these areas of common interest when you are negotiating on your own behalf. If you were representing or advocating for an outside company or business interest, it would be easier to handle the natural obstacles that come up. You would have the luxury of maintaining some distance between the issues and your personal reactions.

You almost need to approach the job offer experience as an "out-of-body" experience, pretending for a moment that your job is to be an advocate for yourself.

Step 2. The next step accomplishes this by helping you sort through and prioritize the personal issues from the career/business issues. Use the following chart to capture information as you go along. Think about what you want in this position. If it is positively charged (+) and personal, list it in the personal column and put a check mark in the (+) column. If what you want is a professionally driven or career/business issue, list it in that column on the chart and indicate whether it is a (+) positively charged issue that should be easy to address or a (−) negatively charged issue that will require a great deal of planning and might generate resistance from the employer.

Refer to the chart on page 188 often as you proceed through the discussion.

Step 3. Review your resume and isolate the items that the employer has identified as a *match* for what the company needs. A "match" would be a good, strong connection between what the employer needs (to have problems solved) and the skills and capabilities you can offer. It is these areas of match that will give you the most objective and powerful data points from which to negotiate.

Step 4. Remain close to the concrete reasons the employer is interested in you and you will find it easier to stay on track in the

PERSONAL AND CAREER/BUSINESS ISSUES

+	–	Personal	Career/Business
✓			Salary level
✓			Benefits
✓			Healthcare
	✓	Amount of vacation time	
	✓		Child care
	✓		Elder care
✓			401(k) plan
	✓	Flex time	
✓		Telecommuting 1 day per week	
	✓		Lower percentage of travel

negotiation process. The chart on page 189 is another tool to help you stay on track. Put the position specifications and your resume in front of you, and as you outline the needs and requirements of the employer in the left column, fill in your accomplishments and skills that correspond to what they are looking for in the right column.

MY PROFESSIONAL QUALIFICATIONS (SAMPLE)

Employer's Needs and Requirements	My Professional Accomplishments and Skills
7–10 years' related experience.	12 years' related experience.
Bachelor's degree.	Bachelor's degree.
Advanced degree preferred.	Master of Science degree.
Leadership experience on teams.	6 years' leadership experience in a team setting.
Experience with large-scale capital projects.	5 years' project management experience.
15%–20% travel.	
Strong, demonstrated platform skills.	Recognized for my ability to design and deliver effective presentations to all levels.

MY PROFESSIONAL QUALIFICATIONS

Employer's Needs and Requirements	My Professional Accomplishments and Skills

In the preceeding chart, list the requirements or specifications the employer has outlined in an advertisement or in a position description. Then, list your accomplishments and skills that align with what you have listed on the employer requirements side of the table. Have your resume handy as you complete the right side of your *Professional Qualifications* chart. Be as thorough as possible in your listing of items. You will not only refresh your memory about why the employer is interested in you and the degree of that interest, you will also:

- Organize your thoughts about what their priorities are and, in rank order, how you can contribute to their priorities.
- Become more confident in proceeding with the negotiation.
- Have targeted enough information to use in a tactical way if the discussion becomes heated and you feel stymied by the halt in the process.
- Maintain an attitude of objectivity about your entire career.

PUTTING IT ALL TOGETHER

After you have identified the *common interests* between you and the employer *(Step 1)*, sorted through them and separated the personal issues from the career/business issues *(Step 2)*, reminded yourself about what the employer considers to be a *match (Step 3)*, and used the *Professional Qualifications* chart to align specific ways in which you meet the employer's requirements *(Step 4)*, you need to develop *strategies* and language that will help you stay focused on your marketable skills and professional track record. Each time you observe the discussion becoming difficult for you, remind yourself about the marketable skills and track record you have and make a mental note about whether you're addressing career/business issues or personal issues.

Action Items

_____ Outline personal issues.

_____ Outline career/business issues.

_____ Review negotiation profiles in Chapter 11.

_____ Complete *Personal and Career/Business Issues* chart by listing priorities with an easy-to-deal-with (+) positive charge or a difficult-to-deal-with (−) charge.

_____ Complete the *Professional Qualifications* chart.

Changing the Shape
of the Money

Agenda

- Ranking the eight component categories in an offer.

- Reviewing an offer.

- Understanding the seven measures of an offer.

- Greg's Story *(a newly minted MBA coins a new compensation package).*

- Eleven useful questions for creatively analyzing an offer.

- Outline of two offers.

- Using a Priority Evaluation Matrix when comparing offers.

The power to define the situation is the ultimate power.

JERRY RUBIN
GROWING (UP) AT 37, 1976

Direct compensation is the most prominent part of the offer for most people, but there are many other legitimate measures of the value of the job offer. Figure out how to look at the entire picture involved in the offer. The more you can look at *all* the important aspects of the offer, the more flexibility and creative alternatives you will be able to employ in the actual negotiation process. The eight component categories to pay attention to are shown on pages 194–195. In the boxes underneath each subcomponent, place a "1" to indicate that the component is most important to you; a "2" if it is somewhat important, and a "3" if it is of little importance.

The components of an offer are many. The weighting of each component is a very individual decision. For example, two-career families would value the strength of the partner/spousal relocation and career transition support. This component might become more important than the salary. If the position responsibilities are right, the corporate culture is a good fit, the potential for contributions and professional progression are appropriate, and the base salary is within the right range for the cost-of-living needs, then for a two-career couple, partner assistance becomes more important than a substantial salary increase.

At this point, transfer all of the items numbered ①, ②, and ③ to the list that starts on page 196. As mentioned previously, partner relocation assistance can became a top priority for two-career families. This importance is measured not only in monetary terms, but also in professional satisfaction for both parties in such families. It is no small accomplishment for a professional couple to find two good opportunities in one place.

COMPONENT CATEGORIES OF AN OFFER

① Total Compensation

Base Salary	Medical Benefits	Dental Care Benefits	Vision Care Benefits	Retirement Planning Benefits
☐	☐	☐	☐	☐

② Quality-of-Life Factors

Vacation	Child/Elder Care	Parental Leave Policy	Policy on Telecommuting	Frequency of Expected Relocation
☐	☐	☐	☐	☐

③ Performance Parameters

Performance Expectations	Time Period Associated with Expected Results	Annual Bonus
☐	☐	☐

④ Structure of the Job Position

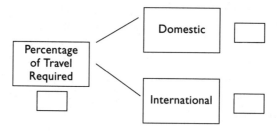

Percentage of Travel Required ☐

Domestic ☐

International ☐

⑤ **Resources and Support Available**

Technical Support	

- Information Systems
- Engineering (if applicable)
- Research and Development

Interdepartmental Support	

- Marketing
- Accounting and Finance
- Customer Service

⑥ **Employer's Commitment to Career Development**

Tuition Assistance	Professional Development and Support	Mentoring	Coaching

⑦ **Perceived Stress Level/Time Investment**

Peak Work Hours	Parental Leave Policy	Policy on Telecommuting	Frequency of Expected Relocation

⑧ **Employer's Show of Goodwill to Ease Transition**

Relocation Package	Sign-On Bonus	Partner/ Spousal Assistance	Job/Career Assistance

Relocation Assistance

MOST IMPORTANT PRIORITIES OF AN OFFER/ASPECTS OF THE OFFER

_____   _____

_____   _____

_____   _____

_____   _____

_____   _____

_____   _____

_____   _____

SECONDARY PRIORITIES/ASPECTS OF THE OFFER

_____   _____

_____   _____

_____   _____

_____   _____

_____   _____

_____   _____

LEAST IMPORTANT PRIORITIES/ASPECTS OF THE OFFER

_____   _____

_____   _____

_____   _____

_____   _____

_____   _____

_____   _____

CREATIVELY CHANGING THE
SHAPE OF THE OFFER

This point in the negotiation process is where you can exercise the greatest amount of creativity. Creative solutions come out of a solid understanding of the following seven facets of the process.

Seven Measures of an Offer

① All the facts of the offer:

a. Total Compensation *(factoring in the value of employee benefits)*

Base Salary

Medical benefits

Amount of contribution

Coverage for self

Coverage for family

Health club benefits

Dental care benefits

Amount of contribution

Coverage for self

Coverage for family

Vision care benefits

Amount of contribution

Coverage for self

Coverage for family

Retirement Planning Benefits

401(k) plan (tax advantages)

Profit-sharing plan

b. Quality-of-Life Factors

Vacation and personal time allotments

Child/elder care

Parental leave policy

Philosophy/policy on telecommuting

Pattern or frequency of expected relocation

c. Performance Parameters/Evaluation Mechanisms

Performance expectations

Time period associated with expected results

Annual bonus

d. Structure of the Job/Position

Percentage of travel required

Domestic

Foreign

Reporting relationship

Formal

Dotted line

e. Resources and support available

Technical support

Information Systems

Engineering *(if applicable)*

Research and development

Interdepartmental support

Marketing

Accounting and finance

Customer service

f. Employer's Commitment to Career Development

Tuition assistance/reimbursement

Ongoing professional development support and training

g. Perceived Stress Level/Time Investment *(will vary greatly with level)*

Peak work periods

Overtime hours typically worked

Amount of additional work probably required at home

h. Employer's Show of Goodwill to Transition *(especially if physical move is required)*

Relocation package *(could write a chapter on this alone!)*

Spousal assistance

Job placement

Other

Sign-on bonuses *(not related to relocation)*

② The motivations, needs, and goals of the employer.

③ What is most important for you about the offer *(e.g., the most important terms of the offer, the second most important terms of the offer, and the least important terms of the offer (see Chapters 1, 2, and 4).*

④ Your Negotiation Profile *(Chapter 11).*

⑤ The employer's Negotiation Profile *(e.g., the way an employer represents the company throughout the interview process should give you clues about probable scenarios during the negotiation process, (see Chapter 11).*

⑥ What you are willing to compromise around or make trade-offs between *(e.g., being willing to trade off a higher salary for an additional week of vacation).*

⑦ How to discuss the areas of compromise and trade-off in ways most relevant for the employer's needs and priorities *(see Chapters 5, 9, and 10).*

Establishing a grounding in these seven areas will empower you to measure every angle of the offer, to effectively manage the negotiation process, and to creatively introduce the trade-offs you want to bring about.

Greg, a professional in the midst of a career change had serious reservations about his ability to realize any changes in his offer package, but he decided to take the counsel outlined in this book and tried his hand at negotiation. Here is his story:

GREG'S STORY

Greg had worked in the public sector in Washington, DC, for several years. His professional track record was strong and impeccable. For his field of program and policy analysis, he had reached the top level in his agency at the ripe age of 27. He had enjoyed his work and colleagues, but he wanted to continue the exciting pattern of growth that he had experienced in his five years' work with the federal government.

As he evaluated his talents and skills, he decided that what he most enjoyed was the ability to analyze trends, programs, and strategies and systematically find opportunities for increased effectiveness or profitability.

For 10 years, he had entertained the idea of going to graduate school to get an MBA. He decided to apply to business schools and was accepted. He knew that he would have to make adjustments in his approach and characterization of issues because the style and language used in the public sector would differ from that of the private sector. He welcomed the chance to make the shift from government work to private enterprise and regarded the MBA as his "credibility and validation" ticket of entry into another part of the professional world.

Greg successfully completed his coursework in the MBA program and with a major in finance, launched into interviews with representatives from the financial services industry in New York. He received job offers for analyst positions and was faced with making a choice. The two offers included the following components:

Offer 1	Offer 2
$62,000 base salary	$65,000 base salary
$5,000 hiring bonus	No hiring bonus
$5,000 year-end bonus	$2,400 year-end bonus
Full benefits	Full benefits
1-week vacation	1-week vacation
No relocation assistance	Relocation assistance

Greg liked both firms equally. He knew that the pace of work and the pressures involved in working in the financial services industry would be intense and with the offers in hand, he realized that he had ignored quality-of-life priorities. Not only was he launching into a new career, but he was also moving to a new city and was in a serious relationship that he wanted to formalize. What a lot of change to deal with all at one time!

Greg evaluated both offers and used these eleven questions to creatively analyze the structure:

① What could replace a higher salary?

② Could they be flexible with a telecommuting arrangement?

③ In what way could I present trade-offs so that they might restructure some aspects of the offer?

④ What has their experience been with the restructuring of offers?

⑤ Are they wedded to a certain kind of offer?

⑥ What would make them invest in a certain kind of job offer structure or format?

⑦ In what areas might they consider changes?

⑧ Are they dealing with the issue of internal equity?

⑨ Are they dealing with corporate tradition or history?

⑩ How can I find out about ways in which they might be flexible?

⑪ How many alternatives can I come up with such that they might be willing to change?

Greg thought through each of the eleven question areas and decided to concentrate on these areas:

① *An additional week of vacation.*

② *Relocation assistance.*

③ *The possibility of telecommuting one day per week.*

He presented the three areas in the following way: He would like to accept the offer, but would like an additional week of vacation (for a honeymoon), $5,000 for moving expenses, and one flex day per week for telecommuting.

Response from Firm A (Offer 1)

Firm A would be willing to put Greg on the payroll one week early for "project start-up" related work rather than give him monies for relocating. They did not want to set a precedent for dispensing a relocation allowance because they hired a significant number of people each year and they had not incorporated relocation into their recruitment and staffing budget.

They were willing to consider an additional week of vacation and were willing to discuss a one day a week telecommuting arrangement at the time of Greg's six-month performance review.

Response from Firm B (Offer 2)

Firm B agreed to trade off the year-end bonus for an additional week of vacation but would not agree to telecommuting. They had had bad experience with telecommuting and had decided to suspend that practice.

Greg decided to accept Offer 1 from Firm A. He felt that they showed more flexibility and concern in the way they responded to him. Though he had to prove himself for six months before he would be given the additional week of vacation time, he felt confident that he would perform either at or above the expected level.

Greg used the Priority Evaluation Matrix as he weighed the two offers. The results of Greg's evaluation of the two offers are shown on pages 204 and 205. The instructions for using the matrix are shown on page 203.

You may want to complete your own *Priority Evaluation Matrix.* The instructions that follow on page 203 will enable you to interpret the sample matrices for Greg and then to fill in the matrices provided at the end of the chapter. This exercise will help you determine how well an offer meets your individual needs.

It's easy to lose sight of the quality-of-life implications of a job offer. The first impression about an offer is normally based on the salary, the benefits, the title, and location. It is common to let these few data points drive the evaluation and negotiation process. The problem is that if your assessment of the composition and value of the offer is based on only a few items, you are more likely to back yourself into a corner. Your potential employer may be less reluctant to provide fringe benefits and perks that would be more valuable to you personally than increased salary and bonuses. The more exhaustive you are in your appraisal of the offer, the more alternative approaches you will have to work with.

Consider the full range of factors involved in the offer when you determine whether to pursue it.

Priority Evaluation Matrix

Instructions

Column	
① *Factor*	List the aspects of an employment offer that mean the most to you. Several common factors are preprinted. Add others that are meaningful to you, up to a total of 10 (add more if necessary).
② *Ranked Priority of Factor*	In the second column, rank each factor from "10" for highest importance to "1" for the least important factor.
③ *Offer*	In Column 3, record data for the offer you receive, either in monetary terms or in a few descriptive words.
④ *Satisfaction Index*	Judge how well each item meets your needs. A "10" indicates that the offer meets your needs perfectly. A "1" or "0" shows the opposite. (Do not rank order from "10" to "1." You may have several 10s or none—imagine yourself as a gymnastics judge!)
⑤ *Column 2 times Column 4*	Multiply the numbers in Column 2 by those in Column 4. The resulting number is an evaluation of how each of your concerns is being met, prorated by the importance you place on the factor. Rating an offer in this way provides a reasonably objective evaluation of how an offer meets your primary concerns.
⑥ *Comments*	Personal notes.

Rating an offer in this way provides a reasonably objective evaluation of how an offer meets your primary concerns. Totaling the numbers in Column 5 will provide an overall rating for the offer. Include your reactions to each specific item.

Blank matrices on pages 206 and 207 are for your use, to compare offers from two employers or a first and second offer from a single employer.

GREG'S OFFER 1
PRIORITY EVALUATION MATRIX

Factor	Ranked Priority of Factor	Offer Data	Satisfaction Index	Column 2 × Column 4	Comments
Salary	8	62,000	9	72	Good salary
Bonus	3	5,000 + 5,000 year end	10	30	Good bonuses
Fringe Benefits	4	Full	10	40	Fine
Amount of Travel	6	Fine	10	60	I'm okay with this
Performance Expectations	9	Okay—Good	8	72	I can perform well
Medical Benefits	2	Good benefits	10	20	Fine
401(k)	1	Good	10	10	Okay
Relocation Allowance	7	None offered	7	49	I would recoup this in my bonus
Telecommuting	5	Okay	6	30	Okay for later
Vacation	10	Okay	9	90	I want more
TOTAL				473	

GREG'S OFFER 2
PRIORITY EVALUATION MATRIX

Factor	Ranked Priority of Factor	Offer Data	Satisfaction Index	Column 2 × Column 4	Comments
Salary	8	65,000	10	80	Good base salary
Bonus	3	None for hiring Bonus 2,400 year end	3	9	No bonus is fine—year end bonus good
Fringe Benefits	4		9	36	Good package
Amount of Travel	6	Acceptable amount of travel	9	54	Acceptable to me
Performance Expectations	9	I am fine with them	10	90	I can do this job well
Medical Benefits	2	Good benefits	10	20	Good benefits
401(k)	1	Okay	1	1	
Relocation Allowance	7	Fine	0	49	They are creative with this
Telecommuting	5	Under consideration in 6 months	0	5	
Vacation	10	1 week	8	80	I hope to get more time later
TOTAL				424	

Priority Evaluation Matrix

Factor	Ranked Priority of Factor	Offer Data	Satisfaction Index	Column 2 × Column 4	Comments
Salary					
Bonus					
Fringe Benefits					
Amount of Travel					
Performance Expectations					
Medical Benefits					
401(k)					
Relocation Allowance					
Telecommuting					
Vacation					
TOTAL					

PRIORITY EVALUATION MATRIX

Factor	Ranked Priority of Factor	Offer Data	Satisfaction Index	Column 2 × Column 4	Comments
Salary					
Bonus					
Fringe Benefits					
Amount of Travel					
Performance Expectations					
Medical Benefits					
401(k)					
Relocation Allowance					
Telecommuting					
Vacation					
TOTAL					

Action Items

**Check
When
Completed**

_____ Rank the eight component categories of an offer.

_____ Evaluate the important priorities of an offer.

_____ Review the *Seven Measures of an Offer.*

_____ Read Greg's Story. Address the *Priority Evaluation Matrix* for Greg's offers.

_____ Fill in the *Priority Evaluation Matrix* with information from your offer(s).

Wealth is the product of man's capacity to think.

AYN RAND
THE NEW YORK PUBLIC LIBRARY BOOK OF 20TH CENTURY AMERICAN QUOTATIONS, 1996, STEPHEN DONADIO, JOAN SMITH, SUSAN MESNER, AND REBECCA DAVISON, EDITORS, NEW YORK: THE NEW YORK PUBLIC LIBRARY

PART 3

AFTER

Bringing Closure to the Negotiation Process

| CHAPTER **20** | *Diplomatically Turn the Offer Down or Confirm Acceptance of the Offer* |

Agenda

- Make sure to repeat your understanding of the position and the terms of the offer.

- Express *(verbally and/or in writing)* your appreciation for their time and for the quality of the dialogue.

- If you are declining the offer, state your reasons in a positive, constructive way.

- If you are accepting the offer, make sure that you or the employer outlines the terms of the offer in writing.

Far and away the best prize that life offers is the chance to work hard at work worth doing.

THEODORE ROOSEVELT

Date: Today

To: Those of You at the Critical Last Juncture

Subject: How to Turn an Offer Down in the Right Way and/or
         How to Confirm Acceptance

The closing of the negotiation process requires the same sensitivity as all the earlier phases. Just because you are completing this process, doesn't mean that everything will become simpler. The careful handling of the ending negotiations can either result in a respectful difference of opinion and a formal, cordial close or, if the offer is accepted, a strong and constructive beginning to a new relationship. If you turn the offer down, keep in mind that it is a small world. The likelihood that your path will cross with that of the person who has offered you a job is high. You will want to leave things on good terms. You might find the person who offered you a job contacting you for another opportunity, referring you to another company and opportunity, or serving as a networking source.

Whether you decline or accept the offer, take special care and conduct yourself well. You might be tempted to be expedient at this point, but you have reached a definitive juncture in the negotiation process, and it needs its own attention and careful handing.

- First, make sure that you have probed every aspect of the offer and have not relied on assumptions. Go through a final quality control audit to ensure that you have examined every possible way to reach agreement:

QUALITY CONTROL AUDIT

① Did the process break down or did we reach an impasse? _____

_____

② Was there anything I could have said or done to continue the process or to have created a different result? _____

_____

③ Were the trade-offs too large to reconcile? _____

_____

④ Did I think clearly and thoroughly throughout the process or did my emotions enter into the discussion and cloud my thinking? _____

_____

⑤ Did I do enough homework; did I gather enough factual informa-. tion to support my requests to the employer? _____

_____

⑥ Is there anything I should have known that would have made me more effective in the negotiation process? _____

_____

⑦ What kind of negotiating style or profile do I have? _____
What are my strengths? _____
What are my weaknesses? _____

⑧ Did the employer come to the negotiation with experience in the process? _____
Was the employer comfortable in his/her role? _____

⑨ Did I help create the right atmosphere for an open, effective exchange? _____

_____

⑩ Was I creative in my way of developing alternatives? _____
Could I have done better work in this area? _____

⑪ Was I effective in separating the personal issues from the professional or business issues? _____

_____

⑫ Was there anything I could have done to change the offer that I wasn't sufficiently prepared to carry out? _____

_____

- Second, if you decide that the offer is not right for you, *decline with careful, thorough attention to the relationship.* If you are not aware of the intricate nature of having to decline an offer, you might find that a groundswell of disappointment builds up between you and the employer.

A great deal of energy and effort is spent both by you and the employer to get to this final phase in the career search or career change process.

An example of a well-written letter declining an offer is reproduced on page 214. Be sure to respect the time which they have put into the process. Though the offer might not be appropriate for you, the interest they expressed in you is worth a great deal. In essence, you have someone or a group of people who believe in your professional capabilities. Safeguard and cultivate the relationship that has begun—*it is a rare and valuable commodity.*

The employer will feel let down regardless of what the circumstances involve. You might also feel somewhat disappointed. You can neutralize the employer's disappointment somewhat by recognizing aspects of the business or organization that impressed you. Suggesting another strong candidate for the position can also be helpful in offsetting this disappointment.

The relationship with the employer begins when they first contact you for an interview. As their interest in you increases and as your investment of time, preparation, and interest increases, the relationship is strengthened.

Making an offer to a candidate represents a significant commitment of time and resources and, if the employer is sufficiently savvy and sophisticated and handles each step in the process with the right amount of care, it will take some time to solidify the relationship. The flow of the contact might look something like the graphic on page 215.

Each negotiation is slightly different. The dynamics, details, and important turning points change from one discussion to another. But, if you remain attentive to separating the relationship issues from the professional, job-related issues, you will find it more manageable to maintain a civil and satisfying exchange.

Diane Nelson
Director, Information Systems
Riggs Corporation
222 South Broad Street
Glasswood, OH 43215

Dear Diane:

Thank them for their time, their hospitality, the offer, etc.

Thank you for having spent such an extensive amount of time in the interview process, and for the offer of employment. It was impressive to meet with you and your staff in the Information Systems department. They were eager to share information about the successes in the department and

Compliment them on an aspect of their business or staff, if appropriate

quick to recognize your lead role in the installation of the companywide system.

It is with combined gratitude and regret that I must decline your offer. As I mentioned on the telephone, I have been in the midst of final discussions with two other companies. On Monday, I declined a second employment offer and accepted the offer I think is best suited for my professional goals.

Describe in general terms the reasons(s) you are declining the offer

Difficult though it was, I accepted this third offer because of the unusual chance to create an Information Systems department. The resources and personnel will be made available to establish a state-of-the-art Information Systems function.

If possible, offer to support them by recommending someone

During the past five years, I have been very active as a member of the Executive Committee for our professional association. I have become acquainted with several association members who would make strong candidates for the position I was offered. I would be most willing to facilitate introductions between you or I would be willing to share information about these individuals with you.

Thank you again for extending the offer to me. It was

Close by expressing your gratitude for the offer

difficult to make a decision and the degree of difficulty has been symbolic of the strength, viability, and promise represented in all the offers.

Please feel free to contact me at (666) 444-9999 if you would like the names and telephone numbers of the individuals in our professional association. I wish you continued success and look forward to our paths crossing in the near future.

Cordially,

Linda Marks

Anatomy of the Employer ←→ Candidate Relationship

Stage of Relationship	Employer Focus	1st Meeting (1–1.5 hours) → Polite questioning: Who are you? → One or more interviewers	2nd Meeting (several hours) → Probing for a real match between need and capabilities	3rd Meeting Offer (1.5–2.5 hrs)	Final Meeting Yes/No
Relationship is getting established— they need a lot of data	Interview screening *(low risk and low investment)*	↑			
Relationship is of medium strength— there is a great deal of evaluation going on	In-depth interviewing *(low to medium risk for the employer—medium investment)*		↑		
Relationship is strongest at this point because the employer is ready to make an offer	Interview → turns to validation meeting to test the strength of the match *(high risk and investment)*			↑	
High risk for employer and for you. Best meeting if you have prepared and the risk is a calculated one	Final discussions about the offer—you decline *(see letter in this chapter)* or—you accept *(see letter in this chapter)*				↑

The number of meetings you might have with the employer could vary. The important things to pay attention to are:

- The ease of communication.
- The number of individuals from the organization you have met.
- The amount of positive momentum that has taken hold.
- The degree of interest they have shown in you as a candidate.
- The strength of the fit between your background and their needs.

As you proceed toward the decision to accept the offer, refer to the following quality control audit:

① Did we leave anything undone or unclear (e.g., discussing any details of the offer)? _____

_____

② Is this offer at least 60%–70% right for me? _____
  Why? _____

③ Can I make valuable contributions to this organization? _____

④ Can I grow with this organization? _____

⑤ Do I think I can respect the people with whom I will be working?

_____

⑥ What do I think will be my biggest challenges in this position?

_____

_____

⑦ What are the important issues in the department, division, and company?_____

_____

⑧ What will my role/responsibility be in addressing these issues?

_____

_____

⑨ What will be important for me to be successful and how can I efficiently establish that? _____

_____

After you have answered these questions to your satisfaction, consider the example offer letters on pages 218 and 219.

Offer letters vary in length and detail. If you are not satisfied with the phrasing or content of a letter, *do not* sign it. Have the employer change it or verbally agree to the necessary changes and initial the changes. The letter should serve as a clear, correct document that can be a point of reference for both parties as you progress into the employment contract.

If you will be going to work for a smaller company, you might have to provide the written version of the terms of agreement. Leave space for you and the employer to sign and date the letter. *Remember,* putting this information on paper will ease your entry into the organization. You will find it easier to separate business agreements from personal issues if you can go back to the original terms outlined in a letter.

SAMPLE LETTER OF ACCEPTANCE

Dear _____

This letter confirms my acceptance of the _____ position. My salary will be $ _____ and I will begin employment on _____ , _____ . Benefits include: _____ , _____ , _____ , _____ , and will take effect on: _____ . Thank you for the offer. I look forward to working with X organization.

Date: _____   Date: _____

Your Signature: _____   Employer Signature: _____

Dear Peter:

We are pleased to offer you the position of Senior Analyst with our firm. A position description is being updated to reflect our discussions. Pending your review, agreement, and signature, we can close this phase of our selection process.

You will report to Kim Jones, the Director of Business Development, and will serve as a member of a 5-person team. Your compensation will be $70,000 per year, and you will receive a $5,000 hiring bonus. Six months into your assignment, we will conduct a performance appraisal and, depending upon the review, you will be eligible for a 5%–10% bonus.

Salary is an indicator ONLY

Please discuss our benefits plan with Phil Jameson in Human Resources. You can reach Phil at 333–4422. Most of the benefits will commence on your first day of employment with us.

We look forward to your arrival on July 15. The members of the group you interviewed with extend their welcome to you and look forward to working with you.

Please do not hesitate to call me if you have any questions. Please sign the attached copy of this letter signifying your acceptance and return it to me by July 1.

Yours truly,

Lynn Johnson

Accepted: _____

Signature: _____

Date: _____

Dear Joan:

We are pleased to extend you an offer of employment. Your title is in the review process, and we will, hopefully, have made the change in position specifications and title within the next week.

Your salary will be $60,000 per year with a 10%–15% annual bonus and stock options. We will send you a full benefits description under separate cover and will ask that you work with our Human Resources Manager on the details of our cafeteria-style benefits plan.

After one year, you will be eligible to participate in our profit-sharing plan.

Due to the nature of our work, we ask you to sign a Confidentiality Agreement and return it to us by Friday, October 7. We also ask that you verify your work authorization status within three days of your employment with us.

The team is looking forward to your arrival. Don't hesitate to contact me if you have any questions.

Sincerely,

Barbara Fisher

> Salary is
> an indicator
> ONLY

Accepted: _____

Declined: _____

Signature: _____

Date: _____

Action Items

**Check
When
Completed**

_____ Review your *Quality Control Audit* questions
and answer them.

_____ Generate a list of terms if you are accepting an
offer and make sure you have outlined
everything.

_____ Make sure you are making the right decision by
checking the offer against your core criteria.

_____ Confirm your offer acceptance or offer decline
in writing.

*What a beautiful fix we are in now; peace has been
declared.*

NAPOLEAN BONAPARTE, 1769–1821
AFTER THE TREATY OF AMIENS, 1802

APPENDIXES	*What Negotiation Looks Like for Each of the Audiences*

Agenda

I. From Interview to Accepted Offer: A Final Overview of a Successful Hiring Process

II. "Transitioned Out": How to Cope, Enlist Support, and Transition Back into Action

III. For Graduate Students in the Negotiation Process: Extra Homework to Leverage Your Degree and Special Skill Sets

The following three Appendixes supplement the information imparted and exercises recommended in the main body of the book. The first appendix, "From Interview to Accepted Offer: A Final Overview of a Successful Hiring Process," examines the offer stage in the broader context of the complete hiring process; the second, "Transitioned Out": How to Cope, Enlist Support, and Transition back into Action," examines the formidable challenges and possible triumphs for individuals who have involuntarily disengaged from their organizations. The third appendix, "For Graduate Students in the Negotiation Process: Extra Homework to Leverage Your Degree and Special Skill Sets," offers perspectives and strategies for the master's program student about to enter the even more advanced arena of job offer negotiation.

Take what is appropriate and of interest to you out of each section and feel free to integrate specific ideas and action steps into the main chapters of the book as you see fit. I hope that these additional ideas will help energize your individual negotiation process and produce long-term positive results.

Appendix I

From Interview to Accepted Offer: A Final Overview of a Successful Hiring Process

What does a smooth, effective negotiation about a job offer look like? What are the reasons why you might experience success and why you might run into trouble?

You might be surprised to learn that *the process* does not start with the first words exchanged across a conference room table or long distance by telephone. It begins with the impressions created when you first meet the potential employer. Key dynamics are set in motion during that first meeting.

FIRST IMPRESSIONS

The first interview is the time and place for establishing groundwork. Both parties form impressions about how easy or difficult it is to communicate and to arrive at a common understanding. The words that are used, the body language that exists, and the atmosphere that is created result in either an easy and natural flow of information on both sides or a stilted, cumbersome exchange of information.

YOUR GOAL

As a candidate, your goal should be to cultivate an open, friendly atmosphere so that you can share as much information about your accomplishments as possible.

RULES OF THUMB

Some important rules of thumb to use during the first interview are:

- Approach the interview as a two-way *(not a one-way)* exchange.

You	The Employer
Have accomplishments, a professional track record *(supported by references)*, credentials, and a base of demonstrated skills to offer the employer.	Has a set of problems to solve and a preconceived, predetermined compensation package associated with creating the solutions to these problems.

- Identify the 5 to 10 achievements you want to promote and exemplify.
- Be prepared to give specific examples to illustrate the impact of your accomplishments. Create a clear understanding in the mind of the interviewer about ways you can contribute to the organization.
- As you discuss your accomplishments, *check* your understanding and assumptions of what the employer is looking for. Avoid making the mistake of promoting the *"wrong accomplishments"*; that is, those that are not directly relevant to the company's needs.

QUESTIONS YOU COULD ASK THE INTERVIEWER

① Please describe the successes your organization has experienced in the past several years and why they occurred.

② If you were to outline the most significant challenges that have to be addressed in this functional area, what would they be and why?

③ How would you describe the skill set needed for this position?

④ How has the person who most recently occupied this position handled the job? What was his or her emphasis?

⑤ What results would you like to see from the person in this position?

⑥ What appealed to you about my background?

When you confirm that you are on the right track, go into an accurate, positive description of your achievements and promote yourself. After you have established the first impressions and have gotten on the right track in the interview, you need to pay attention to, and help set in motion, the steps that immediately follow the interview:

- Ask the interviewer to describe the process they are using for screening candidates for the position.
- Ask what the time frame is for the initial interview process.
- Before leaving the interview, politely ask whether you should contact the company and, if so, in what time frame, or if the company will contact you, and in what time frame.
- Write an interview thank-you letter within a week of the interview (see the example on page 226).

SECOND INTERVIEW

Usually, you will have another interview if you are a strong candidate. The process will most often involve two (or more) interviewers, in either back-to-back interviews or group interviews. In both cases, ask for names and functional titles and/or areas of functional responsibility before the interview begins.

This is a formative part of the interview and subsequent negotiation processes. Pay close attention to the atmosphere in which the interviews are conducted. Observe the dynamics between the interviewers and listen carefully to the questions each person asks. The way your questions are handled is of critical importance, as is the way in which you are given access to core information about the position for which you are interviewing, or the department you would be working in, the division or area you would be a part of, and the company at large.

Sensitivity to the three main dimensions of this process is essential:

① The *people.*
② The *business process/*the *work.*
③ The *culture/environment.*

AN INTERVIEW THANK-YOU LETTER

253 Jaguar Lane
Harrisburg, PA 22522
(715) 299–6666

April 4, 1999

Ms. Pat Long
Director, Human Resources
Enervex, Inc.
595 Strasse Lane
Wienerbrad, PA 22691

Dear Ms. Long:

Thank you for the interview on Tuesday, April 2, at 10:00 A.M. I believe that the match between the needs of the position and my experience and accomplishments is very good.

I appreciated the opportunity to discuss my background. The possibility of working for Enervex at this important stage in its development is of great interest to me. Please extend my appreciation to your staff for the professional, courteous way in which I was treated.

As discussed at the close of our meeting. I will contact you in two weeks to inquire about the next step in the hiring process. Thank you again for a very informative interview.

Sincerely,

Susan M. Brown

The more data you can get from each of these areas, the better equipped you will be to handle the later aspects and dynamics involved in the negotiation process.

After the second interview, you will probably have a clear idea about whether you will get an offer of employment. Make sure to write an interview thank-you letter to everyone with whom you interviewed and send it within a few days. The same *rules of thumb* followed during and after the first interview will need to be followed at this juncture.

Assuming you receive an offer, prepare yourself for the following:

- You will probably receive an offer over the telephone.

- You should also receive a written version of the offer. If the employer is a small company, you might need to write a letter in which you state the terms of the offer as you have heard them—and ask the employer to indicate agreement by signing it.

If you find a discrepancy between what has been offered and what you would like to realize, you will need to go through the process outlined earlier in this book. If the difference between what they are offering and what you would like is significant, you will need to *carefully* plan ways to try to close the gap.

If you have only minor things to reconcile, you will still need to be careful and prepared. Use the following guidelines:

TWELVE-POINT NEGOTIATING CHECKLIST

**Check
When
Completed**

_____ ① Sit down face-to-face, reiterate why you are interested in the offer and the employer, and review each part of the employment offer. Ideally, you are with the person who has the power or authority to change the offer. If not, *try* to get that person involved.

_____ ② Identify areas where disagreement exists.

_____ ③ Prioritize the areas that need to be discussed according to the amount of possible difficulty involved with each area.

_____ ④ Begin discussing the first area—select something that can probably be changed fairly easily. Positive momentum will take hold in the negotiation if you begin with something easy.

_____ ⑤ Remember to separate the person with whom you are negotiating from the issues you are discussing. Be careful and gentle with the person and be clear and tough with the issues.

_____ ⑥ Proceed to the next issue and present what you understand about the terms as stated by the employer. Collect more information about the term under discussion. Remain focused on the business part of the discussion and use open-ended questions to gather more information from the employer about why the offer was structured the way it was.

_____ ⑦ If you resolve the terms, proceed to the next item. Be mindful of the need to allow for give-and-take in the discussion. If you can give a little on your side, it might be easier for the employer to give on that side.

_____ ⑧ If you find that the discussion becomes difficult and heated, try to postpone the remainder of the discussion and set up another meeting.

_____ ⑨ If you can go through the terms that need to be discussed and finish the negotiation in one meeting—do so. At the end of it, make sure to put the final terms of agreement in writing.

_____ ⑩ Thank the person(s) with whom you have negotiated. Many people are not experienced in negotiation and could have experienced some uncertainty and discomfort in their ability to manage the process for the employer.

_____ ⑪ If you have not been able to reach a satisfactory resolution of issues, and you have exhausted all your prepared alternatives, politely end the discussion. Write a follow-up letter emphasizing your appreciation for the offer and for the interest they had in you. Also state your disappointment that a mutually satisfactory agreement could not be reached.

_____ ⑫ If you have reached a satisfactory resolution, offer to write a letter outlining the points of agreement, your start date, and your title and salary. Emphasize your enthusiasm in starting to work for them. Alternatively, the employer may prefer to revise or restate the offer.

These are only some highlights of a relatively straightforward, uncomplicated negotiation. Not all negotiations go this smoothly. It is important to realize that the success of a negotiation is subject to many factors. The personalities of all persons involved in the process play a major role in the flow of the discussion and the successful resolution of issues.

Many factors influence the flow, dynamics, and success of a negotiation. Each negotiation is slightly different. The process is one of the most dynamic forms of communication and information exchange. Pay close attention to the following key variables and work through the steps in this book to keep you grounded and boost your confidence in ways you might never have thought possible.

Key Variables in the Negotiation Process

- The conditions under which the negotiation occurs (environment, amount of time permitted, time of day, etc.) can make a great deal of difference in the way in which you experience this process. These conditions play a significant role in the way a negotiation will progress; for example, if your peak energy period is the early morning, try to arrange your most critical discussions during this time period.

- The amount of experience the employer has in the art and process of negotiation. The employer's expertise will significantly influence the success of the process.

- The timing in which different issues are brought up (e.g., creating and building positive momentum by prefacing a difficult issue with an easier one). The rhythm and pace of discussion can affect the results of negotiation.

- The amount of authority the person you are negotiating with has to change the offer. The less authority the person has, the more the process can be impeded and the more cumbersome the discussion can be.

- The amount of frustration you, the candidate, experience and the way in which you handle the frustration. Everyone has a slightly different tolerance level for frustration, which can influence the negotiation process.

- The homework you do as the candidate. If you are hasty and haphazard in your preparation, you will probably regret it during a process like this.

- The precedent that has been set for negotiation. If the employer has negotiated as a common practice and is not surprised by the need to discuss the terms of the offer, you will find the process goes more smoothly.

Action Items

**Check
When
Completed**

_____ Remember that the negotiation process begins with the very first interview!

_____ To best prepare for the all-important interview, review your accomplishments and phrase them from the employer's perspective. Write down probing, open-ended questions that will elicit substantive information you can use in the negotiating process.

_____ Write and mail a thank-you letter within one week of the initial interview.

_____ If you are invited back for a second interview, continue to gather data from the employer and focus on three main areas: the people, the work, and the culture. Write a thank-you note, as before, to each person who interviews you.

_____ Once you receive an actual offer, both oral and written, review and utilize every step of the *Twelve-Point Negotiating Checklist.*

_____ Keep in mind that every negotiation process is unique—stay grounded, prepare, and feel confident in your newly acquired negotiating skills.

No one can make you feel inferior without your consent.

ELEANOR ROOSEVELT, 1884–1962, FORMER FIRST LADY,
AMERICAN HUMANITARIAN AND DIPLOMAT,
CATHOLIC DIGEST, AUGUST 1960, P. 102

Appendix II

"Transitioned Out":
How to Cope, Enlist Support,
and Transition Back into Action

Thousands of professionals make significant career changes every year. The number of companies undergoing reengineering has created a climate of career turmoil and uncertainty for employees. All levels of workers are being affected by the massive restructuring waves that have swept across the United States.

The workers, whether exempt or nonexempt, have found themselves in the unfortunate position of having been *transitioned* out of their organizations. The euphemistic descriptions used to talk about the circumstance of unemployment, all translate into the same language of jobless anxiety and usually lack of preparation for the demands of today's job market.

Today's job market requires a high degree of sophistication. The more fortunate among this population receive transition support and outplacement assistance. Whether support is offered or not, the tests to the downsized person's skill, stamina, and psychological fortitude are frequent and unyielding.

CONFRONTING AND SURVEYING
THE INEVITABLE STAGES OF JOB LOSS

If you have or are going through a job loss situation a common experience is, a cycle of grief stages—from *shock* that this has happened—to *anger* at the people who were responsible for causing this to happen—to *bargaining* to try to change the reality—to *acceptance*.

The stages in this cycle do not ebb and flow in tidy, compartmentalized ways. The reactions that typically go with the downsizing experience vary in intensity and duration. All of us respond to grief in our own way and at our own pace. It is predictable that more than once, each of the grief cycle stages will dominate your thoughts and emotions. If you are not careful, some of your behavior will reflect negative and counterproductive aspects of your experience.

Too often, people who have experienced job loss as a result of organization downsizing catapult themselves into the job search process before they are intact, ready, and focused on what they need to do to effectively make the transition to a new job. Out of a knee-jerk reaction to reincorporate a sense of order, stability, and control in their lives, people often rush into a frenzy of sending resumes and letters out for position openings.

A definite sense of relief takes hold when resumes are sent out and when positive responses come back. But unless job seekers are grounded in what is of fundamental importance to them, the force and momentum of the responses will distract them from their priorities. It is very challenging to face the realities, emotional upset, and jolts to self-esteem that job loss causes. The strongest people often find themselves on an emotional roller coaster.

STARTING TO BUILD A NEW FOUNDATION

When you enter your job change process, you will be well served if you shore up your network of support and if you build organization and structure into your process. Two experiences that most frequently impair people in career transition are:

① Feeling disconnected or alienated because they have lost their connection with colleagues, their work, and a big part of their identity.

② Feeling out of control.

Because the structure imposed by the workplace is no longer available, a vacuum is created and a replacement structure is needed. If you are not oriented toward developing schedules and maintaining a list of goals, actions, and deadlines, you might want to enlist a colleague or friend to serve as a coach. You might also use the following tool:

PRIORITIZED GOAL AND TASK LIST

Sample Goals	Tasks and Subtasks		Completion Deadline
Attend professional association meetings to cultivate a network.	Find 2–3 appropriate associations.	Consult membership chairperson for each association and get schedule of meetings.	Within the first month of the job search.
	Contact the area chamber of commerce.	Find out about conventions, trade shows, or information fairs worthwhile attending.	Within the first month of the job search.
Exercise 4 times per week.	Meet with JP to walk 5 miles on Monday, Tuesday, Thursday, & Friday.	Begin morning exercise regimen.	Ongoing (begin immediately).
Call 7 employers from last week's mailing to cultivate interest.	Make calls each morning to try to set up interviews.	Send follow-up note and an appropriate article.	Ongoing.
Determine core priorities for type of work.	Identify type of office environment you want.		Ongoing (begin immediately).
Add Your Own Goals			

Practice Pays: How to Rehearse for the Actual Negotiation Conversation

As you progress through a job search, should you reach the point of weighing an offer and arrive at a decision to negotiate, you probably will feel at a disadvantage because you were let go by a company. It will be vital for you to be armed with:

- A clear grasp of what is important to you.
- An understanding of your market value.
- A well-thought-out strategy and tactical plan for the negotiation.

Most importantly, to offset some of the natural and strong emotional reactions to your previous job loss, immunize yourself with thorough preparation and planning. Follow the steps in Chapters 1 through 20 and engage a friend or former colleague in a series of practice negotiation sessions. A script for one of the practice sessions could look like this:

Employer: Jim, we would like to offer you the job. The compensation is close to what you were making before you were let go from your last company.

You: Thank you for the offer. Can you tell me more about the details of the compensation and benefits structure?

Employer: Well, Jim, our Human Resources Manager can give you better information about the benefits. I came up in salary as high as I could go.

You: I can appreciate the challenge of trying to arrive at an appropriate level of compensation.

Employer: Yes, I have internal equity issues to pay attention to as well as an overall companywide wage structure and salary grades to work with.

You: If we were to look at other ways to incorporate an increase, in what way could we do that?

Employer: I am really not sure what you mean?

You: Could we agree on my attending two professional development conferences?

Employer: Of course we could work that into the budget since it comes out of a different part of the budget. I have a little bit of flexibility with this area of expenditure and would not have any difficulty justifying this.

You: The cost of two conferences plus airfare and hotel would help in closing the gap between what I was making and what you are offering. The information and networking would be valuable to the company and to me in making the transition.

Employer: We want you to join our organization, and we want you to feel satisfied and well treated. I am glad we have come to an agreement.

You: Thank you. I feel good about the offer. I know that I will be able to contribute in the priority areas discussed in the interview process. I also think that it would be good to schedule a three-month review and a six-month review. At that time, if I am performing at or above the stated levels, could we build in an incremental increase?

Employer: I don't see why not. I will work that into the employment agreement letter that I will draft for you.

You: I will be ready to start working for you after I have had a chance to review the benefits. Could I meet with the Manager of Human Resources in the next couple of days?

Employer: Yes. I will call her right now and will have her call you this afternoon.

You: Thank you very much. Barring any questions about the benefits, I look forward to starting at the beginning of next month.

Employer: Thank you. I will send the job offer letter to you by the end of this week. We look forward to having you on board.

Pay special attention to how you feel as you go through a role play of a negotiated exchange. Stop when you feel uncomfortable and take notes about your reactions and feelings. Resume and stay focused on how well you are able to remain clear and on track. Insert different responses or challenges as you progress through the exchange. The more you rehearse, the more comfortable you will become in developing new alternatives. Use the following chart to chronicle your reactions *and* your progress:

ROLE-PLAY REVIEW SHEET

Subject	My Response	Desired Response	Next Steps/ Preparation
Start date for new job.	I understand your need for me to begin on that date, but I am not available for another month.	Thank you for the offer. It is good to think about joining your team. I have to bring closure to two other commitments, which will take approximately three to four weeks. I want to begin working for you without any interruptions.	Practice Practice Practice
		Add Your Information Here	

Action Items

**Check
When
Completed**

_____ Keep a daily chronicle or journal of your reactions to your situation.

_____ Use tools to help you stay organized and on track.

_____ Generate a list of supporters and canvass your network for people who are good influences or persuaders.

_____ Be patient with yourself if you are weathering the blows of grief from a downsizing.

_____ Practice mock negotiating terms of agreement with a friend or former colleague.

I wish to preach, not the doctrine of ignoble case, but the doctrine of the strenuous life.

THEODORE ROOSEVELT, 1858–1919,
26TH PRESIDENT OF THE UNITED STATES,
SPEECH TO THE HAMILTON CLUB, CHICAGO, APRIL 10, 1899
(*WORKS*, MEMORIAL EDITION 1923–1926, VOL. 5)

Appendix III

For Graduate Students in the Negotiation Process: Extra Homework to Leverage Your Degree and Special Skill Sets

As a graduate of a professional master's program, you have developed habits of studying, evaluating, and processing information that lend themselves well to negotiation. As a graduate student, you were trained to slow down and isolate important information and work with data. Problem solving is a big part of the preparation and analysis phases of graduate study and also of the negotiation process.

What you might have gotten from your graduate program:

- An ability (or tolerance) for *learning* about something in which you have little interest. Knowing how to learn information is not automatic. If you have had to discipline yourself to concentrate on subject matter that does not hold your interest, you can apply yourself in working through the steps in this negotiation process. There will, undoubtedly, be steps you are not as motivated to work through, but your sense of self-discipline will help you.

- *Research* skills are a basic part of advanced education. Not only might you have an ability to locate information, but an ability to ask the right *questions.* It is no small task to identify the appropriate questions. When you are appraising your market value, the strength of your research skills will be useful to you *(see Chapter 6 for specific suggestions on researching your market value).*

- *Analysis* is fundamental to graduate education. Whether you have to analyze concepts, ideas, and theories, or numbers, equations, formulas, and hypotheses, your skill in dissecting the whole of something into smaller, more manageable pieces is an **essential** skill to have in this process. If you exercise the habit of asking questions rather than resting on assumptions, you will be more likely to get accurate, reliable information.

- *Self-presentation* comes into play in almost every graduate program. Formal group presentations, thesis defense meetings, case reviews, and seminar presentations give you opportunities to work on your ability to communicate clearly in front of a group. Most of your presentations will have been based on research and preparation, but you also have to field questions that might require flexible, creative, and spontaneous responses.

  When in a negotiation, you will find yourself going back and forth between clearly thought out answers to questions and exploratory, flexible, and creative responses. The more capable you are in drawing from your previous experiences with presentations, the more confident you will be with this aspect of the process.

- *Working under pressure* is a learned skill. Some people have a natural ability to work well under pressure, but most of us have to learn how to stay focused and organized when pressure builds. You will find that if you have learned how to handle getting projects, research papers, or reports in on time and have simultaneously handled several priorities, you will be able to transfer this ability to the negotiation.

  Pressure mounts as you think about presenting yourself and your interests. It can also be challenging to handle the pressure of conflict or disagreement during the negotiation.

- *Problem solving* will work very well for you. In your graduate program you have had to solve either practical problems or abstract, theoretical problems. The methodology you had to follow forced you to use order and probably logic. Among the best ways to master the negotiation process is to anticipate and plan for the possible problems that will arise. If you follow a well thought-out methodology as you plan for how you will approach each type of problem, you will find yourself well prepared and more composed during the discussion.

- *Calculation* of alternatives and trade-offs is critical in this process. Focus on the quantitative analysis part of your graduate work and ways to efficiently measure the value of something. Transfer this skill to your calibration of your market value and the comparative value of an offer. Make sure to do your research when you determine your value and look at all the aspects of the offer.

Important advantages you will have are:

- A practiced ability to break down the process into workable pieces.

  Value: *You will appear more prepared than the average negotiator.*

- A tendency toward analysis of information and organization of your thoughts.

  Value: *You will come across with more conviction than the average negotiator.*

- An ability to convey your ideas with clarity and logic.

  Value: *Your communication skills will make it easier for you to handle difficult questions.*

- An energy and enthusiasm that comes from having completed another credential.

  Value: *You will have a fresh perspective and some new techniques to employ.*

Notice how some of these advantages play out in *Barbara's Story*:

BARBARA'S STORY

As a graduate student who juggled completing a degree, holding a full-time job, and making a daily 2½–hour commute, Barbara's stress level was already off the charts when her husband announced that he had accepted a job offer in another part of the country. She would need to accelerate her own job search and refocus her geographic parameters.

Fortunately for Barbara, her master's program had armed her with some of the extraordinary coping skills previously outlined. For example, her acquired research skills and her learned ability to break down barriers to learning something new—in this case, a completely different market—provided a solid foundation for her job search. In addition, her well-honed presentation skills enabled her to connect quickly with a good recruiter in her field and to withstand the grueling pressure of a complex and multistep interview and negotiating process.

Let's see how her story unfolds:

Barbara, a plant manager of a chemical plant, was in the job market because her husband had accepted an offer in another region. She liked her company and her job and was resistant to engage in the job search process. Balancing a high-pressure job, commuting 2½ hours to work and back, and completing a graduate degree filled every hour of her long days.

She was also someone who did not like change and was not comfortable approaching people in her network. Luckily, she happened upon an advertisement for an appropriate level position that was being handled by an executive recruiter. Three weeks after she applied, she received a telephone interview that she carefully prepared for with a long list of examples to demonstrate her professional achievements.

After the telephone screening interview, she was invited for a daylong series of interviews and psychological testing. She had not interviewed for several years and was nervous. She tried to disguise her nervousness by appearing poised and controlled. It was a hard day.

After the day of interviews and testing, she waited for another two weeks to get a clear answer about her status as she was measured against other candidates.

When she got the call that she was going to be invited for a last set of interviews, she was relieved. The final interview stage went well, but the job offer that came through represented a disappointing salary differential.

She responded to the verbal offer by asking for some time in which to think about the offer. During the week she did some research about comparative salaries, benefits, and vacation time and discovered that because of the relocation and the difference in cost-of-living standards, she was probably going to have to take a cut in pay.

When she contacted the recruiter to let her know that she was going to need to negotiate, the recruiter suggested that she work directly with the employer.

Barbara was hesitant to engage in a negotiation process but felt she had to try to resolve some important issues if the position was to be viable.

Equipped with cost-of-living data and comparative salaries for similar positions in other companies in the region, she set up an in-person meeting with the person with whom she had been interviewing.

She presented her concerns in a clear, factual manner and tried to be as calm as possible. Barbara had rehearsed some key phrases and concentrated on using skills she had acquired in numerous presentations at work and in her graduate program.

The person with whom she was trying to negotiate did not have the final authority to change the terms of the offer. As awkward as it seemed, she met with her contact in person and over the telephone four separate times for up to an hour each time. Her contact had to work through his boss who was in another location.

An increase in base compensation, an additional week of vacation time, and an adjustment in the relocation allowance were finally agreed on and Barbara was able to start her new position.

Reluctant as Barbara was to enter the job search, interviewing, and negotiation processes, she ended up doing well. Important lessons from her experience include:

- *Know what you are comfortable with and what you are not comfortable with.*
  Barbara knew that she would not want to immerse herself in a protracted interview process and that she wanted a specific, narrowly defined job search. She also felt that approaching new people would be difficult for her. She wanted to work hard at bringing this offer to closure.

- *Know what your market value is and have concrete data to support your estimation.*
  Barbara was more comfortable with the idea of negotiating with the employer once she was fortified with a lot of data. When she could objectify her request and base it on verifiable research, she was convincing and more composed.

- *Be patient, creative, and flexible. Even after an offer comes through, it is hard to predict how much time it will take for you and the employer to resolve any differences.*
  Barbara had to wait for her request to be presented to a third person in another location and that lag in time extended the process considerably. Be prepared to ask what the discussion might involve and who needs to be involved. Avoid going into the negotiation with rigid expectations.

- *When working through a recruiter, acknowledge that the dynamics in the relationship will be very important in the way the process proceeds.*
  A retained search consultant works for the client, that is, the company seeking the hire. The three-way communication will often take longer, but it can also work to your advantage. You will often have more contact with a recruiter who will be able to share more information about the company and the key leaders in the organization. The recruiter can be a very good advocate for you in this process *(see Chapter 12 for an in-depth look at how professional recruiters can play a role in the interview and negotiating process.)*

Action Items

—————— Identify your unique core skills and abilities as a graduate student.

—————— Identify aspects of the negotiation process you are likely to be comfortable with and why.

—————— Identify aspects of the negotiation process you are likely to be uncomfortable with and why.

—————— Identify resources germane to your field that you could access for data about your market value.

—————— Cultivate a working relationship with someone who could be your negotiation coach and source of feedback.

—————— Complete all the exercises in Chapters 1 through 20.

Man, unlike any other thing organic, or inorganic in the universe, grows beyond his work, walks up the stairs of his concepts, emerges ahead of his accomplishments.

JOHN STEINBECK, 1902–1968
THE GRAPES OF WRATH, 1939, CHAPTER 14

Index